Baseball Drills
for Young People

ALSO BY DIRK BAKER
AND FROM McFARLAND

Teaching Hitting: A Guide for Coaches (2005)

Baseball Drills for Young People:
Over 150 Games and Activities (2002)

Baseball Drills for Young People

More Than 180 Games and Activities for Preschool to High School Players

SECOND EDITION

Dirk Baker

Illustrations by Neal Portnoy
With a foreword by Bill "Spaceman" Lee

McFarland & Company, Inc., Publishers
Jefferson, North Carolina, and London

LIBRARY OF CONGRESS CATALOGUING-IN-PUBLICATION DATA

Baker, Dirk, 1969–
    Baseball drills for young people : more than 180 games and
activities for preschool to high school players / Dirk Baker ;
illustrations by Neal Portnoy ; with a foreword by Bill Lee—
2nd ed.
        p.   cm.
    Includes index.

    ISBN 978-0-7864-3725-2
    softcover : 50# alkaline paper ∞

    1. Baseball for children—Training.   2. Baseball for children—
Coaching.   I. Title.
    GV880.4.B35   2008
    796.357'62—dc22   2008010225

British Library cataloguing data are available

Cover photograph ©2008 Shutterstock

Manufactured in the United States of America

McFarland & Company, Inc., Publishers
  Box 611, Jefferson, North Carolina 28640
  www.mcfarlandpub.com

Acknowledgments

It is the sport that a foreigner is least likely to take to. You have to grow up playing it. You have to accept the lore of the bubble gum card. And believe that if the answer to the Mays-Mantle-Snider question is found, then the universe will be a simpler and more ordered place. — *David Halberstam*

My thanks to my family, Rex, Janeen and Heidi, who have always supported me in every endeavor.

A special sense of gratitude goes out to those individuals whose contributions made this book a reality. They include Neal Portnoy, Bill Lee, Tim O'Leary, Dave Alexander, and Mark Giaquinto.

I want to thank the people who contributed their great baseball and softball drill ideas. In particular, I thank Dave Smith, Bob Casaceli, Rachel Economos, Mike Andrews, Ray Grady, Mike Jackson, Dave Wilbur, John Casey, Rich Gedman, Bob Berman, Leigh Hogan, Pete Wilk, John McGuirk, Greg Desto, and Joe Roberts.

A High-5 goes to the baseball coaches and players at Worcester State College, Boston University, Harvard University, and the folks of Auburn, Mass. You allowed me to live my dream of playing, coaching, teaching, and writing about America's pastime.

Thanks to the people of the Human Movement Department at Boston University who have always inspired my love of writing and the teaching of Physical Education. Special mention goes to Dr. John

Cheffers, Dr. Len Zaichkowsky, Dr. Stephen Ellenwood, Dr. Emily Magoon, Dr. John Yeager, Dr. Avery Faigenbaum, Dr. Eileen Sullivan, Janet Stankiewicz, Skip Farkas, Bill Reilly, Dr. Phil Kelly, Dr. Phil Tate, Jessica Hochbaum, and Dr. Steve Wright.

And in closing, I want to recognize everyone out there who listed "gym" as their favorite subject in school.

Contents

Acknowledgments   v

Foreword by Bill "Spaceman" Lee   1

Preface   3

CHAPTER 1. RUNNING A BASEBALL CAMP, CLINIC, CLASS
     OR PRACTICE: TIPS FROM A TO Z   5

CHAPTER 2. BASERUNNING   23
    The Basics   24
    Team Baserunning Drills   25
    Baserunning Games and Activities   26

CHAPTER 3. BUNTING   41
    The Basics   42
    Team Bunting Drills   43
    Bunting Games and Activities   43

CHAPTER 4. CATCHING   49
    The Basics   50
    Team Catching Drills   51
    Catching Games and Activities   52

CHAPTER 5. FIELDING   55
    The Basics   56

Team Infield Drills   57
Team Outfield Drills   58
Fielding Games and Activities   58

CHAPTER 6. HITTING   87
The Basics   88
Team Hitting Drills   89
Hitting Games and Activities   89

CHAPTER 7. THROWING AND PITCHING   141
The Basics   142
Team Throwing Drills   144
Team Pitching Drills (Overhand)   144
Team Pitching Drills (Underhand)   145
Throwing and Pitching Games and Activities   146

CHAPTER 8. CLOSING WORDS   175

Index of Games and Activities   183

The majority of American males put themselves to sleep by striking out the batting order of the New York Yankees.

—James Thurber

Foreword

by Bill "Spaceman" Lee

To be a superstar and advance to the highest level in the baseball world, you must do four things better than your competitor: field, hit, run and throw. Three out of four will get you a great job at your local Burger King.

Practice must be fun. We will do away with the word *discipline* (sounds too much like whips and chains). We shall substitute the word *play*. Just play. Let's eliminate pressure, also. From now on we don't care who wins and loses. We shall strive for grace, perfect form, a beautiful swing and sound fundamentals.

I learned the game from four great teachers. First among these was my grandfather, who played AAA with the Hollywood Stars. He cut a hole in the center of his glove to develop soft quick hands. I don't recommend this—at least, not until your hands are as tough as Pete Rose's. Second was my aunt Annebelle, who played for the women's professional leagues of the '40s and '50s. She had a great overhand deuce, change of speed and control. Third was my father, who taught me the love of the game. He played for Scotty Drysdale, Don's dad. The credo I played by he wrote on the thumb of my first professional glove: Be smooth, throw strikes, keep the ball down, don't alibi, and hustle, hustle, hustle. My final mentor was my college coach, Rod Dedeaux. His maxim was play not to win, but to play the perfect game.

We won the College World Series in Omaha, Nebraska, and still haven't played that perfect game for him.

Here in Dirk Baker's handbook is a blueprint for practice. Now find an open field and let's have some fun.

Preface

Growing up is a ritual—more deadly than religion. More complicated than baseball. For there seemed to be no rules. Everything is experienced for the first time. But baseball can soothe even those pains. For it is stable and permanent. Steady as a grandfather dozing in a wicker chair on a veranda.—*W.P. Kinsella*

Fantasy camps and old-timer games. Slow- and fast-pitch softball. Rotisserie leagues and pennant races. The "Kids and Kubs" senior citizen softball program or the "Beep Baseball League" for blind players. Roy Hobbs and the "Bad News Bears." Northern games in snowshoes or the Memorial Day Stickball Tournament in Manhattan. San Pedro de Macoris in the Dominican Republic to Wrigley Field in Chicago.

Baseball has been a part of my life for as long as I can remember. It's a great game. One that has basically stayed the same for the last 100 years. It takes tremendous skill to be a good player. But it only takes effort to be called one.

My first baseball experience was "Tee Ball" at age six. In high school I hit over .500, and in college got to play left field at Fenway Park. I coached at Harvard University. I've given baseball talks at camps, clinics and banquets. Two previous books, my doctoral dissertation, and dozens of journalism articles—all centered on baseball. I breathe, eat, drink, and dream about the sport.

Too often people criticize America's pastime, especially at the youth levels. They ask, "Why bother practicing so much? You're never going to be a major leaguer." Don't listen to them. Dream big and go after your goals. There is, however, a method to the process.

My mission in life is to preach the social values of physical education and sport. So many virtues link directly to athletics. Life skills such as effort, competition, sacrifice, work ethic, teamwork, desire, discipline, confidence, hustle and sportsmanship. Just as valuable as hitting a home run is the ability to confront a strikeout head-on. Kids grow up with baseball and softball and thus, we learn how to grow up.

We have fun playing baseball. It's challenging. No one is getting tackled. There is no such thing as a clock. Games can literally go on forever. Anyone can play, and it can be played anywhere. It's the pitcher versus the batter. Will the ball be hit to me? Who made the last out? Did coach call the hit-and-run? So much to think about. So much to worry about. Just awesome games.

Sometimes we forget that girls also play baseball and men often play softball. Most of the games and activities in this book can be applied to both sports. Use them on the diamond, in the gym or batting cage, or in city streets or pastures. Adapt them for any age or team. Teach skills through partner or group work as opposed to working alone. No one fails in a summer camp or pitching clinic. Focus more on enjoyment than on scoring.

I've started with an overview of how to run a camp, clinic, class, or practice in Chapter 1. Each subsequent chapter begins with a basic review of a particular skill followed by a series of group drills, activities and games.

I conclude the book with an important lesson about communication. So much can be gained from personal contact and relationships. Talk to the kids, and make the experience a cherished memory for both them and you. Have fun!

Dirk Baker

Running a Baseball Camp, Clinic, Class or Practice: Tips from A to Z

I ain't ever had a job. I just always played baseball.—*Satchel Paige*

———————————

Many people want to run their own baseball camp or clinic, or just want some ideas for a practice or class. Everyone wonders how to keep kids interested and entertained during that time. This chapter provides tips, suggestions, and ideas to consider for running your own week-long camp, daily clinic, team practice, or physical education lesson plan.

For the camp or clinic, first pick a time frame or week and reserve a facility. Register the camp with the state board of health. Design, print, and mail out a brochure. Hire a coaching staff, trainer and counselors. Generate a name-base, and put kids into teams according to age. Purchase equipment and T-shirts. Type up the daily schedule. Set time limits for each activity. Start with a registration and an opening ceremony. Figure out a plan for meals and injuries. Work on drills and stations in the morning. Play games in the afternoon. Work hard and have fun during the week. Hand out awards and evaluations on the final day. Pay off the bills, and start advertising for next year.

For a practice, devise a daily and weekly schedule. Set a time frame and stick to it. Get more done in less time. Post the goals for each practice. Before it starts have the players dressed and ready to go with the bases in place. Bring a medical kit, the equipment, and water jug. Stretch and throw beforehand. Teach a series of fundamental drills for each position, so the kids can repeat them periodically all season. Make practices a progression (i.e. basic skills to actual games). Continually review and teach new skills. Add in competition and make it fun. Say hello to every kid. Be a hands-on coach. Build camaraderie through partner and group work. If nothing else stay with the old standbys: ground balls-fly balls. Have "dead time" drills such as conditioning or heavy bat swings. Run at the end of practice. Conclude with a huddle, and remind everyone of the next team function.

A suggested unit plan (i.e. six weeks) in a physical education class should include objectives, activities, equipment and evaluation. Plan accordingly for the class size and age group. Memorize the bell schedule. Take attendance. For a lesson plan (daily) state specific goals, equipment, procedures, and evaluation (after completed lesson). Start with techniques, progress to team drills, and conclude with a game. Try nontraditional methods. Use a plan book to record the events and progression of every class. Write down activities which worked and those which did not. Always have a rain schedule. Update and revise every year.

Account

For the class or practice, know the school's budget allocation towards physical education and/or the individual sport. Plan for the short- and long-term. For the camp or clinic, write up an expense account. Figure in camp apparel (T-shirts and/or hats), facility reservation, meals, salaries, mailings and miscellaneous. Photocopy all registration forms and checks. Open a separate checking account. Avoid accepting cash. Have a non-refundable deposit and cutoff date to guarantee a child's spot.

Brochure

Create a colorful camp/clinic brochure on glossy paper. Print plenty of extras. Devise a set of labels on disk. Send out a bulk mail. Ask the area youth league presidents for addresses of the players. Include photos of the director, facilities, and the kids themselves. On the cover include the camp/  clinic name, years of existence, location, age limits, for boys and/or girls, and an address, phone, and FAX number. List facility information, philosophy, dorm and meal info, and a quote from the director. Provide session dates and times, costs (day versus overnight camper), deposit and cutoff date, tuition inclusions (meals, T-shirt, hat, photos, certificate, and evaluation), check-in and pickup times, registration procedures, and the awards ceremony. The player application should include spaces/lines for all biographical information, years of attendance, T-shirt size, day versus overnight, week(s) attending, position choices, parent names, phone numbers, an emergency contact, and how you found out about it. Send along a confirmation notice upon receipt of payment.

Encourage kids to join their friends on teams via the mail registration. Include a separate medical application (week-long) with a standard release waiver, and spaces/lines for a signature and date, insurance requirements, medical information and/or health problems, family doctor and phone number, credit card information, check payable to whom, and the address. Leave space for a "staff use only" section. Another medical form (proof of a physical) may be sent upon receipt of the application. Include a basic daily schedule with times, sample skill sessions and specialties, and day camper information (if applicable). Provide a director biography, staff listing and titles, child-to-coach ratio, family discounts, scholarships (possibly an essay contest), and successes of former campers. One side (address and bulk stamp included) should be left blank for mailing purposes. Advertise on the radio, in newspapers and magazines, on campus email, and in athletic media guides. Hang and dole out brochures at schools, plus youth, summer, and high school games.

Competition

Preach participation and enjoyment over scoring and winning. Stress teamwork over individual performances. Ask the kids to try everything. Bring a bucket of gum to the games, or break out the eye black. Show the kids how to wear the rally hat or helmet. Establish a team motto or nickname such as the Bombers or Wall-Bangers,

Big Red Machine, Cardiac or Whiz Kids, Speed Demons, Arms of Gold, Dirt Devils, or Vacuum Cleaners. Play a game of Ping-Pong or racquetball at lunchtime. Utilize the camp counselors into skills demonstrations. Possibly have a regulation game between the coaches/ teachers and kids. Conclude each day with an enjoyable activity, so the kids are left joyously tired.

Day 1

Start the camp/clinic early with a meeting for both the coaches and counselors. Go over the printed schedule. Then have the kids check-in (overnight versus day camper) at the various stations: dorms, camp store, and the nurse. Set a time frame for registration. Sell any extra T-shirts, but only after each child has received one. Attract a professional player to speak on the first day. Show a video. Make a brief introduction to the parents and kids. Boast of the years of coaching experience and academic/athletic success of the counselors. Move to an evaluation period (week-long camps). Judge the kids (scale of 1 to 5) on baserunning (times), fielding, throwing and batting. End the day with a draft in order to pick fair teams. Record week-long evaluations for pitching, hitting, baserunning, defense, and intrinsic qualities. Leave space for recommendations. Use baseball cards as daily prizes. On the final day have brief closing ceremonies. Bring every child up for his or her evaluation packet, photos (team and individual), and signed certificate. Award an autographed ball by pulling a name from a hat. Ask a major league baseball public relations department to donate leftover promotional items. Pick a Mister or Miss Camp/Clinic (best attitude) for each age group.

Equipment

Use all types of balls and bats. Use the tee for purposes of making contact. Batters and base coaches should wear helmets. Catchers must wear full equipment and a protective cup. Explain the different gloves according to the positions: catcher, infielder, first baseman, and outfielder. Make an equipment inventory checklist. Clearly label all equipment, both personal and team (write names on hats, gloves and

bats). Mark bags with athletic tape according to team names or age groups. For example: Red Sox get the red bags (ages 7 to 8), Blue Jays, blue bags (ages 9 to 10), Pirates, black bags (11 to 12); and A's, green bags (13 to 15). Issue separate bags for the balls (RIF's for ages 5 to 12), bats, helmets, and catcher's equipment. See-through "fishnet" bags are quite durable, reasonably priced, and come in all sizes and colors. Name a "last man" to make sure nothing is left in the dugout. Assign equipment pickup and drop-off to different people each day. Issue a time-limit contest for everything to be picked up or put away.

My preferred equipment includes: Diamond regulation baseballs and softballs, Jugs foam and dimpled balls, Easton Incrediball, Worth RIF Ball, Safe-T-Ball, deBeer Mush Ball, tennis ball, Wiffle ball, handball, racquetball, Nerf ball, Rag Ball, and Rawlings Radar Ball; Easton aluminum bat, Louisville Slugger wooden bat, Easton Thunderstick, Wiffle bat, foam bat, Bratt's Bat, and donut; Jugs or Atec baseball and softball pitching machines and protective screens, Osborne indoor Porta-Mound, LeFebvre or Tuffy batting tees, Shortstroke Trainer, batting cage, Atec soft toss net, Canvas Catcher, and portable hitting backstop; Hollywood anchor and double-safety first base, rubber, strap and breakaway/quick-release bases, home plate, pitching rubber, and chalk; Rawlings mitts and gloves, and Soft Hands training paddle; Diamond catching gear: mask, skull cap, chest protector, shin and throat guards, softball knee pads, plus athletic supporter and protective cup; Rawlings helmets, and Easton equipment bags; Pro Line hats, Rawlings game jersey, belt and uniform pants, Easton or Franklin batting gloves, stirrup socks, Tuff Toe Pro protective cleat mold, Ringor metal spikes, Reebok rubber cleats, liquid pine tar and rag, eye black, stop watch, lineup cards, umpire clicker, scorebook, Gatorade drinking jug, and first-aid kit.

Improvised equipment includes: bat (sawed off broomstick handle or hockey stick), weighted bat (steel pipe), ball (duct tape wrapped around newspaper), home plate (white towel or piece of plywood), bases (deflated bicycle tires), boundary markers (milk jugs), tee (large road cone), and portable backstop (soccer net covered with a tarpaulin).

Facilities

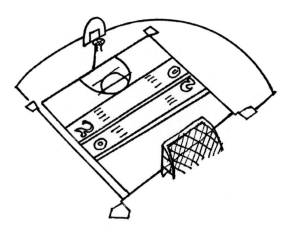

Utilize the pool, Astroturf, basketball court, football field, dugouts and diamonds. Use the PA system and electronic scoreboard for games. Rake the fields before and after playing. Stress respect of the facilities. No food, drinks, sunflower seeds, or gum in the gym, pool, or on the Astroturf. Leave the bathrooms and dorms in better condition upon departure. Throw the drinking cups away.

Goals

Safety is the Number 1 priority in any setting. Skills should be explained, demonstrated, corrected and repeated. Work on the "fun" in fundamentals. Kids should listen and follow the rules. Include everyone. Emphasize the game and not the score. Encourage hustle and teamwork. Remember to smile, and don't be afraid to laugh.

Hitting

Assign a number to everyone. That number becomes a person's slot in the batting order. For a week-long camp, keep the same batting order. The order should continue from the previous spot of the day before. Have one on-deck batter at a time with all other players sitting down in the dugout or bench area. Avoid batting the best players at the top of the lineup to ensure for equal opportunities. For a team intrasquad game try (1) alphabetizing A-to-Z or Z-to-A (last name, first name, etc.), (2) by uniform number, (3) height, (4) position (pitcher bats first, catcher second, etc.), (5) reversing the batting order each day, or (6) the team captains grabbing the bat with fist-over-fist to see who hits first.

For creativity try switch hitting, or make everything a fair ball (except foul tips). Use 3-and-2 counts. Let a toddler stay up until he/she makes contact. Play "Stickball" or bunt with the Thunderstick bat. Use the tee or soft toss (to stress a particular skill) in the actual games as well. When organizing a team-swinging drill in a circle (for safety purposes), put tape on the gym floor (chalk in the parking lot) to distinguish individual "spots."

Indoor Schedule

Always plan for inclement weather. Such a format depends upon the number of kids, gym size, and indoor facilities. Think about lengthening the camp/clinic lunch period, or having extra pool time. Show a highlight or bloopers video. Try a mental preparation/relaxation exercise (confidence building through visualization) with everyone lying down with their eyes closed. Do a "Stump the Coach" trivia extravaganza. Try the "Izzy Wright" (Is He Right?) rulebook quiz. Hold a bubble-blowing contest. Perform softball rally chants. Show the kids how to properly mold a hat, break in a glove, and wear a uniform.

Play the "Alphabet Game" by picking a major leaguer's last name which begins with the letter "A" and so on (go in reverse order for double names such as Andy Ashby). Have a chalkboard session on scorebook symbols and interpretations. Teach the art of signals (verbal and nonverbal). Play "Wiffle ball," "Pepper" or "Flip." Do soft toss or tee work with tape balls. Try one massive "Simon Says" or "Red Light/Green Light" game. And for the hearty during a warm rain storm, go back outside and try a "Rick Dempsey Home Run Trot" around the bases.

                 —Mike Andrews and Ray Grady.

Jersey & Uniform

Print up a quality T-shirt for the camp or clinic, or have an inspirational quote on a team jersey. Create a colorful and distinctive design or logo. That T-shirt is free advertising for your camp, school or program. Administer the shirts according to the size marked on the camp/clinic application form. Make sure every coach, counselor, and staff member receives a T-shirt. Always print up extra. Give shirts out to key personnel such as athletic department staff, janitors, grounds crew, and kitchen workers. Established camps can print up adjustable hats, sweatshirts, uniform pants, or polo shirts for the coaches. Have a day where kids can dress up in uniform of their own local team or favorite professional club. Attract a sporting goods sponsor (i.e. for every 100 T-shirts get one bat free), and print their business logo on the back or sleeve. Some companies run camp/clinic deals: buy a pair of cleats and get turf shoes at half price.

Kinesiology

This term means the study of body movement. Get the kids loose, stretched, and ready to go. Exercises are designed to improve skills and promote better overall health. Stress flexibility and a proper warm-up. Start with a light jog. Progress into stretching, calisthenics, and a group throwing activity. Work together in a circle. Have different leaders each day. Include stretches for the arms, shoulders, wrists, fingers, hips, legs (hamstrings and quadriceps), back, groin and neck. Use calisthenics to increase the range of motion (i.e. jumping jacks, toe touches, bunny hops, low squats, lateral lunges, high knees, backward kicks, skips and carioca). At practice make conditioning a separate station. Samples include pickups and quick-feet exercises (see baserunning section), wall-sits, swinging a weighted bat, squeezing tennis balls, push-ups, sit-ups, reverse dips, jump rope, and medicine ball work. End conditioning, workouts, and practices with a cool-down period.

Lunch

Typically the most popular meal at a camp; have a specific area set up for eating. Stick to the time schedule. Set up tables, chairs and barrels. Have a policy for hot (varied menu) or cold meals (refrigeration). Be courteous in the lunchline. Explain the procedure for serving, sitting and cleanup. Make all meals mandatory. Relax while watching a video. Possibly have a snack time set aside in the morning and popsicles in the afternoon. Bring small snacks (granola bars or animal crackers) along for those long practices or away games.

Making Teams

Arrange the players in a line and have them count off in successive order, "One, two, one, two." Each number is a team. For four teams count off, "One, two, three, four" and so on. Try 10-year-olds versus 11-year-olds, for example. Switch teams regularly, so kids get to interact with a variety of people. Total participation is the key when a team has more than nine players. Thus, have everyone hit in the batting order. Assign people to retrieve foul balls, coach the bases, or keep score. Use more than three outfielders. Designate people to warm up one of the outfielders, the starting pitcher, clean up the dugout area (bats and helmets), or throw balls to the first baseman and center fielder after each inning. Name a head cheerleader or a bench/bullpen coach. Also have people backing up during throwing or fielding drills.

Name Games

Put name tags on people and equipment. Try an "Icebreaker" on Day 1. Sit as a group in a circle. Have each person say their first name followed by an animal which begins with the same letter. For example, "Hello. I'm Dirk the Dingo." The next person should repeat the names of previous people and so on. Adults should help those who get stuck. Then put a ball into play. Pass it left, right or across. After saying your name pass or toss the ball to someone else by first calling out their name. Kids can also act out their favorite position. Follow that up with the naming of their favorite major leaguer; anything which gets the children to speak. As a way to meet new people, toss the gloves into a pile. Pick out a glove which isn't yours, and go speak to that glove's owner for a few minutes. Repeat this activity all week. An instructor should call a child by his/her first name or nickname. Many kids idolize their coaches/teachers, so develop a rapport with them.

Outs

Instead of playing three outs per inning, let everyone bat before changing sides. Use six outs in a group hitting game. Try co-operative play (i.e. everyone touches the ball) to signal an out while the base runner touches as many bases as possible. When "Indian Rubber" is allowed, throws should be aimed below the waist. Encourage catches off of the gym walls and ceilings. In most cases enforce co-operation rather than elimination.

Positions

Get kids to play and learn new positions. For factors of confidence, play without gloves when using a Wiffle, tennis, or Nerf ball. Designate numbers to players on each team, and have them rotate each inning or every two innings. When making defensive changes, simply move players up a number. For

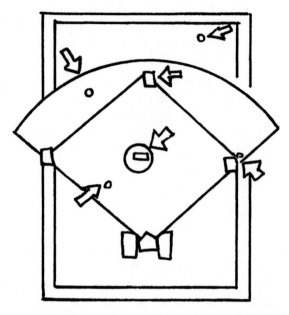

example: The pitcher goes to catcher, catcher to first base, and the right fielder to pitcher. Also, use the short fielder (Number 10). Add a switch with 12 players (bench people), for example, Number 12 would become the pitcher and Number 11 the catcher. Everyone else would move up two slots, and the previous right and short fielders would sit out. Bench players not in the original defensive alignment should bat first. Even if positions change the batting order stays the same. Base coaches should be substitutes or the last two people making outs from the previous inning. When instructors pitch have a kid stand either left or right of the rubber. Let this player field comebackers. Record the alignment of players each day, so children get to play every position.

Quick Rules

The quicker the rules the faster a game starts. Use the "E.D.D." format: "Explain. Demonstrate. Do." When speaking make sure kids look at the instructor with both eyes. Never speak to them until there is complete quiet. Ask kids to repeat the rules. Review skills after stations and games. Hand out pamphlets on the fundamentals. Explain confusing rules such as the infield fly, inside versus outside throws, running in the base line, overrunning first base, leaving a base early, illegal pitch, substitutions, force outs, dead ball, tagging up, out of play, and a dropped third strike versus caught foul tips (high school and up). Make any hazards "out of play."

Instructors should own a clipboard and watch (preferably with a stop watch function). Use a whistle or horn to switch stations. Set up exact time limits, and follow the daily schedule. Allow for stretching, warm-up, time to-and-from stations, and questions. Record game results, and chart progress for evaluations and awards. Alter the traditional rules by allowing fielders to play behind the fence, in foul territory, or behind the backstop. Concessions for age should be made for field size, regulation ball and bat sizes, leading, sliding, length of base paths, plate-to-mound distances, and pitching overhand or underhand. Make creative indoor rules such as home runs off of the basketball backboard or triples which hit specific banners hanging in the gym.

Runs

Instead of running around the bases, offensive teams can do any of the following together before the defensive team records an out or gets the ball back to the pitcher. Try sprinting wall-to-wall, push-ups, sit-ups, or jumping jacks. Skip, hop, or run hand-in-hand with a partner. Allow more than one runner per base. To get more people involved, start each inning with any number of kids on the base(s). Substitute cones as bases. Use a manual scoreboard, or count out loud to keep track of points. Run the bases in reverse, in different order, or vary the direction according to where the ball is hit.

Safety

Create a healthy and safe playing environment. Warm up and condition the kids properly. Review the boundaries. Pinpoint any hazards such as rocks, holes, or sharp edges on the backstop or fences. Avoid dangerous situations altogether. No running up or down steps. Check for untied shoes. Wear cleats outdoors. Remove watches and jewelry. Note that regulation balls, thrown bats, and stationary bases can be very dangerous. Use batting helmets and full catcher's equip-

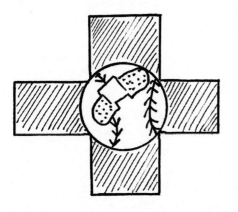

ment. Have the hitting team sit down in the dugout. Make sure the first-aid kit is fully stocked. Know where the trainer or nurse is located and/or nearest phone. Respond to injuries quickly and responsibly. Clean cuts up fast. Young bones break easily, so listen to the kids when they get hurt. Never move anyone who is unconscious. Inform the medical staff of all injuries. A registered nurse or certified trainer should always be on-call.

Hats and sunscreen should be mandatory for any hot weather setting. Have water at every field or station. Be able to notice dehydration and heat stroke. On "3-H Days" (hazy, hot and humid) get into the shade, hose the kids down, or head to the pool early. Every instructor should have a record of child medical conditions (i.e. asthma, seizures, diabetes, allergies, bee stings, etc.).

Toddlers should go with an instructor to the bathroom. Have a lifeguard maintain pool protocol. Take attendance each morning, before and after lunch, and before kids leave for the day. Assign a designated area for "day campers" to stay until they are picked up. Lastly, every instructor or coach should be certified in first-aid and CPR.

The Pitcher

Have a different child pitch each inning. To avoid overuse injuries, find out when kids pitch in their town or city leagues. Use a pitching machine in the batting cage. Have an adult pitch to the younger kids, especially when toddlers have difficulty reaching home plate. Be consistent in velocity. The pitcher can also throw breaking balls (older players), or alter the count (quickens the game).

Umpire

Every game should have an umpire and strict rules. Encourage questions beforehand. Use a clicker to keep track of balls, strikes and outs. Any arguing or questioning of calls should result in a lost run for that particular team.

Variety

Camp, for example, is a great experience for the coaches and counselors too. Adults want to learn new drills and rekindle old friendships. Encourage people to get involved with stations they have little or no experience in. Challenge the kids to learn new skills, and help those less talented. Change stations from week to week. Ask coaches to wear their school T-shirts and the many varieties of minor and major league caps. Bring along wooden bats and the fungo. Dare to do what no camp has done before. Take a day trip to a nearby minor league game (group ticket deal). Document the many moments on a video camera. Record the kids on video during the hitting, pitching, and fielding stations, then analyze their strengths and weaknesses. Include a visual teaching station by showing them action photographs of the big league ballplayers. Arrange the album according to hitters (stance and swing), pitchers (grips, release points, and follow through), catchers (framing and blocking), throwing (arm angles), fielding (diving, grounders, and fly balls), and baserunning (sliding).

Work

While camp or class is fun for the kids, it's also work for the instructors. The coaches/teachers should run the teams, stations and games. Have the counselors umpire, throw batting practice, and feed the pitching machines. Start each day with a theme. Let the staff offer Game Day scenarios, fundamentals and drills. Devise a salary scale, and tell each staff member his/her pay check amount before Day 1. Increase pay for exemplary work, years of service, and inflation. Include stipends for gas (commuters) and dorm supervisors. Award checks on the final day. Pay the staff generously. A camp/clinic is only as good as the people who work at them. This includes directors and assistant directors, coaches, counselors, trainers, nurses, and guest speakers. Hire experienced youth, high school, summer, and college coaches. Attract enthusiastic teenagers from the local area. Send information along on designer letterhead to the staff during the year (include a phone/mail directory). Notify them months ahead of time about the camp/clinic dates.

X

Never put an "X" through a kid in relation to effort. Everyone deserves a chance to perform. Discipline is another story. For effective learning to occur, the instructor must have control of the playing environment. Be fair and consistent, and never pick favorites. Be courteous and polite. Foul language is forbidden by everyone. Use positive reinforcement. Avoid using running as punishment. Threats rarely work, but taking away what kids enjoy most (games) can be very effective in controlling rambunctious youngsters. Notice if a kid is just having a bad day or isn't feeling well. Talk to them and find out what's wrong. Show them that you care. Troublemakers may surface, so deal with them swiftly and decisively. Avoid holding a grudge, but know that "one bad apple can ruin the crop."

Yard

Play on the big or little diamonds. Drive vans to local fields. Create multiple diamonds on the Astroturf or football field. Organize small stations throughout the field. Put bases down in the gym. Assemble batting tunnels and mini-cages in areas out of the way. Run hitting stations in the parking lot. Set up a pitching station (throwing targets) against a cement wall.

Z's

A key to athletic performance is a good night's sleep. For overnight camps assign two counselors per floor with 2-to-4 kids per room. Have a lights-out policy (depending on age) as well as an orientation on Day 1 (i.e. rules, emergency procedures, and locations of the cafeteria, nurse's station, and pay phone). Coaches should stay in separate quarters.

A suggested overnight camp clothing list includes the following: fan, pillow, sheets, blanket, pajamas, watch, alarm clock, sneakers, shoes, socks, underwear, pants, shorts, shirts, sweats, bathing suit, shower shoes, jacket, rain coat, laundry bag, towel, toiletries and case, sunscreen, bug repellant, all baseball/softball gear including glove, bat, hat and cleats, equipment bag, water bottle, reading materials, walkman and headphones, pen, notebook, postcards, stamps, flashlight and money. Label clothes and equipment appropriately.

Baserunning

When I was a small boy in Kansas a friend of mine and I went fishing. I told him that I wanted to be a real Major League baseball player, a genuine professional like Honus Wagner. My friend said that he wanted to be the president of the United States. Neither of us got our wish. —*Dwight D. Eisenhower*

THE BASICS

Running

Run on the balls of the feet, and pump the arms up and down. On infield grounders run hard past first base. Turn right after hitting the bag. On base hits make a cut to the right halfway down the baseline, and hit the inside corner of the bag. Watch for signals when on the base. Focus on the pitcher while getting a lead (baseball). Get a low/wide stance, and dangle the arms between the legs. Stand about three big steps away from first base. After the pitch, hop aggressively off of the base; this is called the secondary lead. On the steal, swing the left arm across, cross over, and head straight to the next base. (In Little League and softball, lead from the crouched or sprint position facing the next base with one foot on the bag.)

Look to advance on a steal or wild pitch, and never go if you hesitate. With zero or one out(s), take the lead at second base in the base line. With two outs, get behind the bag and advance on contact. Get a good secondary lead after the pitch. At third base take a lead in foul territory then move towards home plate on the pitch. The runner should also listen and watch the base coaches. Show the number of outs, and pre-think the situation. On-deck batters should communicate to scoring runners.

Sliding

On close plays slide about eight feet before the base. Drop onto the rear end. Keep the front leg straight and foot pointed in the air. Bend the other leg under the straight one. Keep the arms in the air. Use a bent front leg and the body's momentum for the pop-up slide, and advance to the next base if the ball gets away. Try to hook the leg to one side in order to slide away from a tag. Slide headfirst on steals. Clench the fists when diving. Always slide into the base on force plays. Never barrel over a catcher. Avoid sliding into first base unless there's a high throw.

TEAM BASERUNNING DRILLS

Age: All.

Object: Work on the techniques and body movements according to each base.

Equipment: Bases.

Rules: Use the double-safety first base for younger players; one each for the runner and fielder. Start with simulated plays (i.e. steals) or half-sprints, so the group can repeat the

skills over and over. Save the full-sprint for when proceeding to the next base or station. Always use actual bases when outdoors, and have an instructor stand at each bag (issue penalties for missing). Go individually home to first one after the other; groups of three for the other bases. Change the situation after everyone has gone. Add in right- and left-handed pitchers (baseball) plus offensive signals. Modify the below techniques according to the age group and sport.

Home to First

1. *Infield Grounder:* Take a full swing, and make a quick look for the ball. Run through first base, and turn right after the bag. Challenge the kids to run in a straight line on the actual chalk.

2. *Base Hit:* Take a full swing, and make a quick look for the ball. After

seeing the ball go through the infield, make a wide cut to the right and come hard across first base.

First to Second

1. *Leads:* Shuffle off about three big steps. Stay low and balanced. Get a secondary lead after the pitch is thrown.
2. *Steal:* Shift sixty percent of your weight to the right leg. Thrust the left arm towards second and cross over. Stay low.
3. *Hit-and-Run:* Same as the steal play except make a glance into home plate about halfway between second base.

Second to Third

1. *No Outs or One Out:* Shuffle off about four steps in the base line. Get a secondary lead after the pitch is thrown.
2. *Two Outs:* Shuffle off behind second base. While in the secondary lead get a good break for third base upon contact.

Third to Home

1. *Wild Pitch:* Shuffle off about three steps in foul territory. Get a secondary lead after the pitch is thrown. Score on a wild pitch, or else hustle back in fair territory.
2. *Squeeze Bunt* (Baseball): Shuffle off and break for home when the pitcher's front foot touches the ground.
3. *Sacrifice Fly:* On a fly ball to the outfield, hustle back with the left foot on the base. On the catch, cross over and score.

BASERUNNING GAMES AND ACTIVITIES

Touch 'Em All

Age: All.
Object: This is a simple drill to get a group warmed up.
Equipment: Four bases.

Rules: Start everyone at home plate at about 5- to 6-foot intervals apart. Jog around the bases. Make sure to touch each bag. No passing. Go four times around.

Touch Base Relay

Age: All.
Object: Knock home the importance of touching the bases in this fun race.
Equipment: Four bases.
Rules: Make four equal teams. Have each group standing up in a line behind their own designated base in the infield grass. The formation should look like the letter "X." At the starting signal, the first person in each line runs to the next base. You must touch each of the four bases, and then sit down at the end of your line. Each person then moves up a spot. If anyone misses a base, that particular team is eliminated. The first team to have everyone sitting down is the winner.

—Keg Wheeler and Otto H. Spilker, *Physical Education Curriculum Activities Kit* (New York: Parker Publishing Company, 1991).

Scamper

Age: 6 years and up.
Object: This is a relay race for running around the bases.
Equipment: Two cones, two balls, home plate, and four bases.
Rules: Make two teams, each with a ball. Everyone starts at home plate with two distinct lines behind two cones. Use two second bases with Team 1 touching the one closest to home plate, and Team 2 touching the one closest to the outfield. One team goes from third to second to first to home; the other first to second to third to home. After each run the ball must be given to the next person in line who then has to run in the opposite direction. Dropped balls, missed bags, or false starts result in five push-ups for the entire team at that very moment. Sit at the end of the line after scoring. The first team to finish wins.

Break the Tape

Age: 9 years and up.
Object: Time and evaluate the speed of each person.
Equipment: Stationary bases and stop watch.
Rules: For running home to first take an actual swing. When touching first base, lean forward as if breaking the tape in a sprinting competition. Don't lunge for the bag. Sprint in a normal fashion. When running first to third or home to home, start from the base or the actual lead. Make a cut out towards right field just before rounding second base. Try leaning to the left when rounding the bag. Be sure to touch every base during the activity. Add three seconds if you miss a base. No sliding. Add in the 60-yard dash for high school and up. Write the times down for each kid, and see if they improve over time.

Starter

Age: 8 years and up.
Object: This is a timed race where runners receive points for their efforts.
Equipment: Whistle, four bases, and four stop watches.
Rules: This game is best suited with either stationary bases or with chalk-drawn bases on a blacktop. Try to use four instructors. Pick four random teams and a captain for each. The captain names a running order which can-

not be changed. Each team then sits down behind one of the bases. At the whistle, the first person in each group runs to the next base. Four bases must be touched. If a base is missed that team is disqualified for that particular round. The instructors (standing together) time one group each. The times are then compared for first place (4 points), second (3 points), third (2 points), or fourth (1 point). Tally up the points after everyone has run, and declare a winner. Play this game each day during a camp, for example.

Bucket

Age: 9 years and up.

Object: Players should "empty themselves" (i.e. a bucket) on the field. From a baserunning standpoint, hustle may even cause an errant defensive throw.

Equipment: Batting helmets and balls.

Rules: Make equal teams. Set helmets up as boundary markers some 10 to 15 feet apart. Place a ball at each. Also have a helmet at the front of each line. Individuals run in order against the other groups. At the starting signal, the first person in each group runs out to the first helmet and retrieves the ball. They then run back to their group's starting point and place the ball in a helmet (the next person in line can hold the helmet upright). The runner then runs out to the next helmet and runs back to their line and so on until all of the balls in his/her line are in the helmet. After the last ball, he/she then sits down at the end of the line. The next runner in line puts a ball at each helmet. Start at the end of the line or at the beginning—whatever the runner wants. That runner is done once all of the balls are at each helmet. Then the next person puts the balls out at the helmets just as the first person did, and so on. Runners cannot begin until the previous runner crosses the starting line. Teams are finished once everyone has gone once and is sitting down.

Dash for Cash

Age: 6 years and up.

Object: The inside-the-park home run is a dream for all hitters. Here players run against a teammate.

Equipment: Four bases plus a home plate.

Rules: Players should pair up with someone according to similar height and weight. Place two bags at second base. The instructor starts the race. One runner heads towards third base and the other towards first base. Race around the bases. Each base must be touched. No sliding into home plate. Runners going to third base should touch second base closest to the mound, and those to first base should touch second base closest to the outfield. The runner who crosses home plate first wins the cash!

Dizzy Bat Race

Age: 9 years and up.

Object: This is a hilarious race based upon speed and balance.

Equipment: Bats and helmets.

Rules: Make equal groups with a starting line and a bat directly in front of each group (30 to 40 yards away). An official should stand at each bat. At the starting signal, the first person in each group sprints to their bat. They must put their hand on the bat and then their forehead on their hand. Spin around the bat 10 times (more spins for older kids). Count out loud for each completed spin. After the final spin, attempt to walk/run back to your team and tag the next person in line. Then sit down. They don't call this the "Dizzy" Bat Race for nothing. Avoid playing this game directly following a meal.

Relay Races

Age: All.

Object: Relay races are fun, competitive, and can involve virtually any number of kids.

Equipment: All depends on the type of relay race.

Rules: Make equal teams. Demonstrate how to use different body movements during the running aspects of the race. Designate starting lines, midpoints, and finish lines with either helmets or bases for each team. Activities could include: crab walks, bear crawls, piggyback races, sack races, leapfrog, standing long jumps, running backwards or sideways, one-legged hops (switch legs at midpoint), and possibly cartwheels. For those all-sports camps, incorporate multiple skills into one race. For example: soccer, basketball, or floor hockey ball dribble, bounce or balance a tennis ball on a racket, or walk with a volleyball between the legs.

Balancing Act

Age: All.
Object: These relay races utilize running and balance.
Equipment: Bats, gloves, bases and balls.
Rules: For each race designate the different teams with starting and finishing points (use bases). In the first game, each kid must run or walk with a bat resting on the end of one or two finger(s). This tests one's balance and hand-eye coordination. Upon arriving back at your team simply flip the bat to the next person. For the daring, then try balancing a bat on each hand. In the second game, race with a ball balanced on top of a glove. After that try to flip the ball up and down off of a glove as you go. For every game, if the object drops to the ground a runner must start again from that point before continuing on.

Pickups

Age: 12 years and up.
Object: This conditioning exercise works on lateral quickness, footwork, and fielding technique.
Equipment: Tennis balls or regulation balls.
Rules: Demonstrate how to field a ground ball. Then space partners about 10 feet apart and facing each other. The tosser rolls a grounder to one side. The fielder shuffles after the ball, fields it with the bare hands, and tosses it back underhand to his/her partner. After catching the ball, the tosser then rolls the ball to the other side. Back

and forth the fielder is shuffling and tossing. Start with 20 each. Make it more difficult by adding another ball, increasing the distances to each side, and lengthening the repetitions. This is a great activity for fielders and pitchers.

Horn

Age: 6 years and up.

Object: Teach listening skills (base coaches) as part of an aggressive baserunning exercise.

Equipment: Whistle and four bases.

Rules: Line everyone up against the backstop or wall. Give each person a number: 1 (first base), 2 (second), 3 (third), and 4 (home plate). One person should start at each base including home plate. Start off in the base-stealing stance. At the starting whistle advance to the next base. At the next whistle kids must decide to do one of three things:

1. Slide into the bag if they're close to the next base.
2. Dive back to the bag if they've just overrun it.
3. Hurry on to the next base if they're somewhere in between.

When each base runner is "safe" on their base, jog around outside of the infield diamond and get back into line. The next four kids then run out to their designated base and wait for the whistle to blow. Encourage diving back into the bags as a way to avoid tags. Finally, as a conditioning exercise use the whistle as a signal to switch directions on the bases.

Speed Trap

Age: 6 years and up.

Object: Teach the art of the rundown, and how to act when you're in a pickle.

Equipment: Fielding gloves, tennis balls, and two bases.

Rules: Explain the roles of fielders and base runners in the event of a rundown. Depending on available space and the number of kids, this game can be performed between first and second base, or between each of the other bases. The goal is for the "police officer" (person with the ball) to catch a "speeder" (person in the rundown). The base runner wants to safely reach one of the bases. An elimination factor can be added here by sending people to the "jail." Those "criminals" include tagged base runners, fielders who collide with a runner, the  fielder closest to a runner who has successfully made it back to a base, or the fielder who makes a poor throw. The "jail" is emptied after each completed rundown since someone is always safe or out. Remember, "speed kills." Steal as many bases and runs as you can!

Department Store

Age: 6 years and up.

Object: This relay race is a great way to end practice.

Equipment: Every piece of equipment which you can find.

Rules: Depending on the total number of individual pieces of equipment, put players on separate teams. Place equal sets of equipment at one end of the race area. For example: Shin pads, chest protector, skull cap, mask, batting helmet, first baseman's mitt, catcher's mitt, batting gloves, bat bag, ball bag, bat, ball, base, tee, etc. Designate the equipment to be worn and where (i.e. shin guards on legs, gloves on hands, and helmets on heads), and which ones can be carried.

    Kids should line up one behind the other. At the whistle, one person from each group runs to the "Department Store." That person wears/carries a piece of equipment back to their team; no particular order necessary. The next person in line then must wear/carry that piece of gear, run and grab another piece of equipment, wear/carry those two items back to their team, and hand everything off to the next person in line. After each person goes, the equipment should be building up over time. The last person should be wearing/carrying everything from their pile. Teammates can help dress each other (i.e. fastening shin guard buckles). A person has to pick up any dropped equipment before continuing.

Wisk

Age: 10 years and up.
Object: Ballplayers should be filthy after sliding and diving, and those "Wisks" around the bases.
Equipment: Throw-down bases.
Rules: Wisk detergent can clean the dirtiest of uniforms. The day before playing "Wisk" tell kids to wear uniform pants, sweats, or old jeans. This activity is best suited without shoes. Start with one giant line of people (standing on the foul line). Have a starting signal. Include five sliding stations.

First, use a peer leader to demonstrate each of the five slides: 1) straight leg but arms down to avoid the tag, 2) pop-up, 3) hook with either leg, 4) headfirst, and 5) slide past the bag and reach around to touch it. Second, have the kids perform each bent-leg slide (leg out front) as a group by pushing themselves along the ground. Third, do each discipline by only taking a few steps and then sliding. Focus on technique rather than speed. Fourth, take a full sprint towards the instructor some distance away. After a sprint, simply turn around and face the other direction. Start off in the stealing position. Fifth, have a sliding contest. Award a prize for the best slide, or give a round of applause to the dirtiest person. On that hot summer day, hose down the "water slide" mat to practice headfirst dives.

Liberty Bell

Age: 13 years and up.
Object: Incorporate the sense of hearing into a baseball hit-and-run activity.
Equipment: Four bases, aluminum bats, helmets and balls.
Rules: Discuss and demonstrate the philosophy of the hit-and-run (stealing second with a quick look into the plate, batter aiming to

hit a ground ball, and runner hopefully advancing to third). Everyone starts at first base. Use a third base coach. Depending on the age (i.e. leads off first base), attempt to steal second against an actual pitcher. The moment the runner looks into home plate, an instructor bangs two bats together (simulating bat-ball contact). Once hearing the ping, the runner should pick up the instructor on what to do: continue onto third (base hit), hold up (pop-up or fly ball), or slide into second (infield grounder). The runner should also slide into second base if he/she does not hear anything at all. This means the batter either swung and missed or missed the sign. End the activity with live batters (wear helmets). First focus on hitting the ball on the ground (swing no matter where the pitch is) then progress to the opposite field. Tips include choking up slightly, using a closed stance, shortening the swing, and swinging down.

Crazed

Age: 9 years and up.

Object: This indoor game teaches aggressive baserunning, the art of the rundown, and force outs.

Equipment: Three gym mats, home plate, rubber ball, and bat.

Rules: Spread the mats across a gym floor for bases. Each hitter has a 3-and-2 count. The defense must stand around the gym with everyone behind the pitcher. At least one player must be playing each infield position including catcher. The instructor is the pitcher and umpire. Outs are recorded just as in a real game. Runs are scored for each base touched, instead of having to touch all four. The base runner must stay on the bag once the pitcher retrieves the ball (i.e. on the rubber). Innings end after the third out. There is no limit to the number of runners on a single base. Advancement is voluntary. However, you cannot pass a runner in front of you. A player is safe while standing on a base. Fielders can tag out any runner with the ball ("Indian Rubber" is allowed with a soft ball thrown below the waist). Force outs can only occur at first base.

Then try this game another way. After a hit, the batter keeps running until hearing "stop." Innings can last for three batters or the entire offensive team. The fielding team must retrieve the ball, everyone must touch the ball and then yell "stop." After a few times around, ask the kids to think of better ways to work together. They first may have thrown the ball to each person. Then someone may have run around to touch each person with the ball. The goal is for everyone to run to the person who catches the ball, form a circle, and for each person to touch the ball. The hitting team (after contact) could also be scoring runs by sprinting wall to wall. Each touched wall is a run. Instead of running do push-ups, sit-ups, jumping jacks, or anything building stamina, endurance and strength.

Vamos!

Age: 6 years and up.
Object: In "Vamos" (Spanish for "let's go") the challenge is to run in the correct direction, not necessarily home to first.
Equipment: Bases.
Rules: Make different baserunning rules for an actual practice game or specific inning. *First Inning:* run the bases in reverse. *Second Inning:* second base becomes first, third becomes second, and first becomes third. *Third Inning:* when the ball is hit to the right side of the field (or infield), the player should initially run to third base and proceed around the bases in reverse. If another batter hits the ball to the left side, then the player runs to first base. If multiple players are on the base paths they must determine the correct direction in which to run, based upon where the ball is hit. Then reverse this trend the next inning. Stipulate that "running in the wrong direction" (for that particular play) results in an out for the offensive team. *Fourth Inning:* refer back to the rules of the first inning. Keep home plate as the final destination in each phase.

Charlie Hustle

Age: 11 years and up.

Object: Compared to his contemporaries, Pete Rose had average baseball talent. With determination, hustle, effort, and courage he became an All-Star at five different positions and broke the all-time hit record in 1985. This activity gets a group into game day shape.

Equipment: Bases.

Rules: When conditioning outdoors, run the bases instead of running around a track or field. Start at home plate (take an actual swing) for each phase. Run aggressively and look to advance to the next base. For example: Think double when hitting a single. First, run through the bag at first base (infield grounder). Second, run home to first (single). Third, run home to second (double). Fourth, run home to third (triple). Fifth, run home to home (home run). After each sprint, jog to the next base(s) until reaching home plate. Remember, as Coach Dave Smith once said to me: "It doesn't take any talent to hustle."

Tic-Tac-Toe

Age: 10 years and up.

Object: These agility drills improve footwork, quickness, balance and stamina.

Equipment: Roll of athletic tape or chalk, and stop watch.

Rules: On the gym floor or in the parking lot, set up a rectangular grid with nine spaces. Hop on one or two feet to-and-from the spaces in the grid. Start off by making the letter "X." Then form the letter "S." Then form these letters in reverse order. Older kids can be taught a specific scenario and compete against the clock. For a simple drill, hop back and forth over a line. First, left and right. Second, front and back. Then hop on both feet while making a small square box. First go clockwise and then counter-clockwise. Then try it on one foot. Use time frames (30 seconds each). Work hard and try to improve the times each day.

—Dave Smith.

Fox Trot

Age: All.

Object: Some of the more famous World Series home run trots include Carlton Fisk's "Get Fair Hop," Kirk Gibson's "Limp" around the bases, Joe Carter's "Get Rid of the Helmet I'm So Happy" jaunt to home plate, and Babe Ruth's "Called Shot" against the Cubs. Here kids can do their own versions.

Equipment: Bat.

Rules: Line up at home plate, and take an imaginary home run swing. Then jog or run around the bases. Go one after the other, or wait for the batter to finish his/her turn. The blast should be deep and be a no-doubter. Be creative and original.

Tools of the Trade

Age: All.

Object: Because diving and sliding are the best places for a uniform to become tangled, stained or ripped, the following activities could be run. Kids should also know the functions and importance of their uniform and pieces of equipment.

Equipment: Hats and uniforms of all kinds.

Rules: First speak about the honor of wearing a team uniform. Take pride in looking like a ballplayer. Appearance is a direct link to confidence. Make sure the uniform is clean for games. Use bleach for whites. Sew up rips and holes. Wear the stirrups correctly. Wear a team T-shirt underneath the game jersey. Button and tuck the jersey inside the pants. Leave the jewelry at home. Avoid batting gloves and wristbands altogether. Shine the spikes. Throw away cracked helmets. Soften a glove with shaving cream, *Leather Food*, or *Neat's Foot Oil*. Break it in by playing catch—not by putting it underneath your mattress. To mold a hat, gently bend/roll the visor on both sides at the same time (no rubber bands). Toss a dirty hat into the washing machine. Some humorous descriptions of the baseball/softball hat include the following:

Michigan Pinch or *Connecticut Roll:* The proper visor mold.

Toronto Maple Leaf: Two or three bends/creases to the visor.

Telescope: Too much curvature to the visor.

Pike's Peak: One crease down the middle of the visor.

Minnesota Flats: No bend at all to the visor.

Tuskeegee Tuck: A hat pulled down over the ears.

Great Dane: Looks as if your dog ate it.

—Hat names: Dave Smith and Bob Casaceli.

Bunting

What's important is that kids discover baseball is fun, and that it gets more fun as you get better at it.—*Mickey Mantle*

THE BASICS

Pivot and Square: When the pitcher breaks the ball from the glove (baseball), open up the hips and stance slightly; this is called the pivot or square (sacrifice situation). The chest should be facing the pitcher and the toes aimed to the opposite field. Slide the top hand halfway up the bat, and grip it with the thumb and index finger. Bend the knees and extend the bat to the front of the plate. Stand balanced with a wide stance. The arms should be both bent and relaxed. The top of the bat should be angled up and just below eye level. Give with the bat on contact in order to deaden the ball. Don't push it. Squat down on low pitches. After contact sprint to first base. Note that bunting is not allowed in *slow-pitch* softball, and is used much more in softball than in baseball.

Sacrifice: Bunt strikes on the ground and away from the pitcher. The goal is to advance a runner(s) to the next base.

Drag: Pivot/square around later than in the sacrifice. Aim to place the ball near the chalk lines. Bunt strikes. Focus on contact before actually running to first base. The goal is a base hit.

Squeeze: Typically a baseball play used in high school and up. Pivot/square when the ball is at the pitcher's "L" (just before release). Bunt anything thrown the hitter's way. Put it anywhere on the ground. The hitter is giving him/herself up in order to score the run. A runner can advance early (*suicide:* when pitcher's front foot hits the ground) or late (*safety:* when ball is on the ground).

Slash: Here the batter fakes a bunt and brings the bat back into the hitting zone. The batter then takes a full swing. The object is to draw the infielders in for a bunt, and then slap a ground ball through the vacated area.

Bunt-and-Run: With a base runner (typically from first base) stealing on the pitch, attempt to bunt the ball towards third base. Use the same pivot/square as the sacrifice. As the fielder throws to first base, the runner heads onward to third.

Fake Bunt: Pivot/square just as in a sacrifice. Bring the bat back quickly (same for non-strikes) just before the ball crosses home plate. This is typically used to take a strike or on a steal situation.

TEAM BUNTING DRILLS

Age: 9 years and up.
Object: Teach the bunt as an all-inclusive drill.
Equipment: Helmets, balls, and bats including the "bunting bat" (wooden bat with a flat hitting surface).
Rules: Explain how bunting wins games. Demonstrate the proper techniques of each phase. Remember that bunting is a hand-eye coordination skill similar to hitting (seeing the ball, hit the ball). Put the kids in lines in front of the instructor. Go through a simulated pitch movement, so batters know when to square around. Then use verbal commands (calling out the various bunts) since each skill calls for different body movements. Progress to bunting groups with a pitcher for each. Issue five bunts per discipline for each person. To end the activity, add in live pitching from the mound with one bunt per person. You can use the "Bunting Bat" for purposes of confidence.

BUNTING GAMES AND ACTIVITIES

Hole in One

Age: 12 years and up.
Object: When putting a golfer must concentrate and use a soft touch. Bunters also need to be confident, relaxed, and place the ball away from a pitcher.
Equipment: Bats, six helmets, gloves, and pitching machine (if possible).
Rules: The instructor can pitch. Hitters receive five bunts apiece depending on the total number of people in a group. First perform the sacrifice bunt, then the drag, and conclude with the squeeze. Attempt to place the bunts into helmets laid out in the infield grass

(three each up the third and first base sides). Scoring includes: 3 points (bunts to the foul line side of a helmet), 5 points (bunts hit-

ting a helmet), and 10 points (bunts going directly into a helmet). Keep track of your own team's score. The bunting team stands in order down the third base foul line (back away from the action). The other team, behind the mound, fields the bunts. A missed or fouled bunt count as strikes. For older players, adjust the pitching machine to curveballs for added difficulty. Also, bunt left-to-right and right-to-left in suc-cession. If bunting indoors, aim the balls towards a corner of the gymnasium for easy pickup. If you have some cones or plastic bot-tles, put six each down the first and third base lines in ideal bunting locations. The bunter receives 12 pitched strikes. See how many cones you can knock over.

Move It

Age: 9 years and up.

Object: This activity combines the many bunting varieties, baserun-ning disciplines, and conditioning.

Equipment: Bases, bats, helmets and balls.

Rules: Pitch from the mound with one person bunting at home plate. Another three people run from each base. On contact the three runners attempt to advance to the next base. The bunter then sprints to first base. A bunter who misses or fouls the pitch off should run to first anyway. Players advance one base at a time. After reaching home, those runners become bunters and so on. No sliding. All participants should be running and bunting at the same time. Move into the next round only after each person has bunted and been to each base. Obviously the runners have different agendas as opposed to the bunters. Work individually on the specific disciplines. Adjust to the age levels. Sessions may include:

Round 1:

Bunter: Sacrifice (run through first base and turn right after the bag).

Runner at First: Steal of second base (work on a quick first step).

Runner at Second: Steal of third base (take a lead in the base line).

Runner at Third: Squeeze (wait for the pitcher's front foot to hit the ground).

Round 2:

Bunter: Drag (simulate a base hit by making a wide cut to the right).

Runner at First: Hit-and-run (midway down the line make a quick look into home plate).

Runner at Second: Steal of third base (start from a 2-out lead behind the bag).

Runner at Third: Score on a wild pitch (sprint from a secondary lead).

Round 3:

Bunter: Squeeze (run through first base and semi-advance on an overthrow).

Runner at First: Delayed steal (take second while in the secondary lead).

Runner at Second: 2-out lead (score on "crack of the bat").

Runner at Third: Score on a sacrifice fly (simulate tagging up).

Round 4:

Bunter: Fake bunt (square around and bring the bat back; then sprint to first base).

Runner at First: Early steal (go at a left-handed pitcher's first move to the plate).

Runner at Second: Wild pitch (advance to third while in the secondary lead).

Runner at Third: Safety squeeze (score when the ball is on the ground).

—George Reidy.

Peas

Age: 11 years and up.

Object: This is a rapid-fire bunting drill designed to get a lot done in a short period of time.

Equipment: Batting cage, pitching machine, Jugs balls, helmets, and Thunderstick bat.

Rules: Use the Thunderstick bat for purposes of hand-eye coordination and confidence. Put the balls into the pitching machine one after another. Stay in the bunting stance for each pitch. Focus on the "peas" shooting out from the machine. Bunt left. Bunt right. Lay down the sacrifice bunt, drag and squeeze. Go through an entire bucket of balls. Don't worry about a pop-up. Get ready for the next pitch, because there's no time to dwell on the negative.

Pinball

Age: All.

Object: Similar to the arcade game of pinball: keep the ball bouncing up and down. Look for bat control and proper bunting technique.

Equipment: Bats and balls.

Rules: While holding the bat with one hand, keep bouncing a ball up in the air before it hits the ground. Use as much space as needed. Holding the bat at the knob makes it more difficult. Make this "the activity of the day," and ask kids to present their highest scores (individual and team) at lunchtime. Bouncing the ball back and forth with a partner (10 to 15 feet apart) also simulates the bunting technique (can use two hands on the bat).

Four-Way Bunting

Age: 12 years and up.

Object: This bunting drill includes bunting and pitching techniques.

Equipment: Bats, balls, bases, gloves, and screens (optional).

Rules: There will be a bunter at each base and one on home plate (four people total). Four pitchers throw to the four different bunters stationed at first, second and third base, and home plate. Either use screens as backstops at the four stations or include four actual catchers in full gear. At a safe distance, line up an equal numbers of bunters at each base. The four pitchers should practice throwing simultaneously. The batters practice their bunting technique (sacrifice, drag and squeeze.) Once the ball is bunted the pitcher should field the ball, while the bunter sprints to the next base (home-to-first, first-to-second, second-to-third, and third-to-home). Work on that quick first step out of the box. Pitchers get an excellent fielding exercise in a live situation (no throwing). They should throw from the stretch, and focus on throwing strikes but they can also add in breaking pitches. Coaches can participate in pitching. To keep score track the number of successful bunts.

—Jay Lavender.

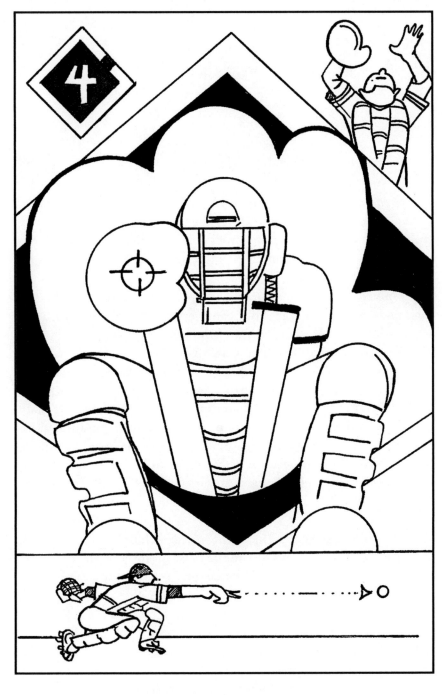

Catching

You gotta be a man to play baseball for a living. But you gotta have a lot of little boy in you.—*Roy Campanella*

THE BASICS

Crouching: Weight should be on the balls of the feet. Sit straight up and close the knees slightly. Give the pitch signal from deep in the groin. Shift to a particular spot well behind home plate. Extend the mitt and give a low target. For protection put the throwing hand behind the shin guard.

Framing: Squat pigeon-toed with a wide base. Be able to slide a chair underneath your rear end. Lean over slightly. Receive with a stiff arm. Don't lunge. Work on turning the mitt up, down, in, and away according to the pitch location. Catch with one hand only.

Blocking: On balls in the dirt, drop to both knees as quickly as possible. Use a quick lateral shift for balls to the left and right. Slide on the pads. Keep the body in front of the ball and square to the plate. Put the glove between the legs with the bare hand behind the glove. There should be virtually no space between the legs. Cup the shoulders inward. Lean out over the ball in order to keep it in front. Bend the head over the ball (to protect the throat). Let the ball hit the chest protector. Never try to glove a ball in the dirt. Lean over more for breaking balls.

After blocking a ball, remove the mask and hustle after it. Assume the throwing position, and square the body up towards the target if a runner tries to advance. If the ball does go to the backstop with a runner on third base, sprint after it, use the pop-up slide, and make a low, quick throw to the pitcher covering. Field ground balls (i.e. bunts) and catch pop-ups with two hands. Have the mentality of blocking everything in the dirt, even with no runners on base. Also, with no one on base back up first on infield grounders.

Throwing: The keys here are footwork and a quick release. First catch the ball, and get a good grip on it. Then take a short jab step in the direction of the target, and drop the back foot. Pretend you're in a hula hoop. After a quick turn and transfer, extend the ball back and up to above the throwing shoulder. The elbow should be bent, facing the target, and just behind the mitt. Make an overhand throw. Release the ball out from behind the ear. Snap the wrist down. Use one step, and throw the ball on a line. Then release the back leg over. Stay low, square, and compact throughout. High school and college baseball coaches look for a time under 2.0 seconds for throws from home-to-second.

TEAM CATCHING DRILLS

Age: 9 years and up.

Object: Design a series of fundamental drills to practice over and over. Focus on technique. Discuss the mental game of calling pitches, taking charge, signaling play calls, and directing the defense.

Equipment: Catcher's gear and tennis balls. Regulation balls for older players.

Rules: Work on different locations and types of pitches. Play with a partner or an instructor. Throw to bases with a hitter standing at home plate.

    1. *Framing I:* No ball; first bare-handed then with the mitt.

    2. *Framing II:* With ball; first bare-handed then with the mitt.

    3. *Dry Jab Step:* Work on the pivot and throwing position.

    4. *Blocking I:* No mitt; balls thrown in the middle.

    5. *Blocking II:* With mitt; balls thrown to the left and right.

    6. *Pop-ups:* Throw the mask and catch with two hands.

    7. *Fielding Bunts:* Throw to third, second, and first base. (Also simulate force out at home and toss to first.)

    8. *Throwing I:* Perform 3 drills: Footwork without throwing, 1-knee quick toss, and no-step throwing drill.

    9. *Throwing II:* Throw from the crouch to third, second, and first base.

    10. *Passed Ball:* Sprint to the backstop, pop-up slide, and throw.

    11. *Tags:* Stand in front of the plate and use a two-handed tag.

Note: When blocking the plate, always keep the mask on.

CATCHING GAMES AND ACTIVITIES

Rain

Age: 9 years and up.

Object: Learn how to find and then catch a pop-up near the home plate area.

Equipment: Full catching gear, mitt, tennis racket, and balls.

Rules: Start from the squat position. Hit a tennis ball with the racket from behind the catcher. Blind to the location of the pop-up, catchers should react when they hear the racket-ball contact or move on a verbal signal. Each catcher gets 3-to-5 pop-ups each. Throw the mask (or use the cap) away from the fielding area only after finding the ball. Make sure your back is to the infield, keep the feet moving, and catch with two hands. It may be easier to catch the tennis balls with the bare hands. For older players, try the ultimate pop-up drill using balls shot out from the pitching machine (tilted on its side). Remember not to panic, because the ball is up there somewhere.

Road Block

Age: 10 years and up.

Object: This is a great game to work on toughness, blocking technique, concentration and endurance.

Equipment: Full catching gear, mitt, bat, tennis or regulation balls.

Rules: Dress in full equipment with or without a mitt. The catcher starts in the squat position behind home plate. Throw or hit balls to the catcher from a close distance away. First practice blocking with tennis balls for purposes of confidence. Then move to regulation balls with easy tosses. Progress to hard throws depending on the skill level. Use rounds of 10 to 20 balls apiece. A successful block is a ball kept in front within a 3- to 5-foot range which the catcher, in a real game, could retrieve and hold a runner from advancing to the next base. Rotate multiple catchers in and out. Those worthy of being called the "Human Road Block" will be loved by their sometimes wild pitchers.

Shin Guard Shuffle

Age: 9 years and up.

Object: Catchers need to think of themselves as a banana: the gear is just an outer layer of skin. These drills focus on getting acquainted to the equipment, footwork, hand-eye coordination, endurance and quickness.

Equipment: Full catcher's gear for each person and balls. For indoor work wear wrestling knee-pads instead of shin guards.

Rules: Have two catchers face each other while standing in a circle. Use the basketball tip-off circle when indoors. While wearing full equipment (no mitts; mask is optional) shuffle around the circle while playing underhand catch with the ball and listening for verbal instructions. The toss should reflect most of the commands (see below). Attempt to frame every toss. Even the catcher without the ball should perform each command. After each skill, continue on playing catch.

Verbal commands include:

> *Left:* Rotate to the left.
>
> *Right:* Rotate to the right.
>
> *Up:* Simulate a pop-up.
>
> *Down:* Simulate a block in the dirt.
>
> *Throw:* Simulate a toss to second base.
>
> *Push-up:* Do an actual push-up.
>
> *Sit-up:* Do an actual sit-up.
>
> *Jog:* Run in place.

Fielding

Baseball to me is still the national pastime because it is a summer game. I feel that almost all Americans are summer people. That summer is what they think of when they think of their childhood. I think it stirs up an incredible emotion within people.—*Steve Busby*

THE BASICS

Ground Ball: Infielders should start in an athletic stance. Be ready for a ball hit in any direction. Lean over on the balls of the feet with the glove extended and open (palm up). Focus on the hitter. When the ball is hit to you, keep the glove extended. Circle and charge the ball. When getting to the ball, bend down (as if sitting in a chair) and reach out for it. The left leg (glove side) should be slightly ahead of the right leg (for right-handed throwers).

The chest should be over the ball. Give with the glove as if catching an egg. The throwing hand should cover the ball once it's in the mitt. Look the ball into the glove, and get the proper grip. Stay low, and bring the ball into the stomach and up to the back shoulder. Pivot the feet and hips around, so the throwing shoulder is facing the target.

Fly Ball: Outfielders should start by facing home plate with their glove on a knee. Sprint after every fly ball. Once the ball is hit, circle the ball so the body is in a good position to catch it. Yell loud for the ball once it's in your sights. Move towards the ball in order to get momentum on the throw. Extend the glove above the head and on the side of the throwing arm. Stand behind the ball, and watch for it over the fingertips. Don't stab at it; let it come to you. Look the ball into the glove, and catch with two hands whenever possible. Get the proper grip before throwing it. Slowly transfer the ball from the glove to the throwing hand. Pivot the body around, and get in a good throwing position facing the target.

Tag: Straddle the bag whenever possible with a foot on either side. Stand ready on the balls of the feet. After receiving the ball extend down with the glove. Attempt to tag the base runner's feet and in front of the base. Don't reach. Tag with the glove-hand only as to protect the throwing hand from being spiked. After a successful tag, get the glove out of the way quickly and look for another play. Shuffle across, in front, or behind the bag according to a poor throw. Remember to always block the ball when getting an out is not a possibility.

TEAM INFIELD DRILLS

Age: 6 years and up.
Object: Learn a series of fundamental drills to practice over and over.
Equipment: Tennis balls and gloves; regulation balls for older players.
Rules: Explain and demonstrate each of the disciplines. Work in groups of two. Start off bare-handed. Then add in gloves and infielder paddles if applicable. Include the following:

    1. Glove Work: Roll balls to each other in the crouched stance with an open glove.

    2. Grounders Straight On: Same as above except start standing up.

    3. Circle: Same as above except circle balls to the left and right.

    4. Forehands: Charge to the glove side, field the ball, and swing the back leg over (as if facing first base).

    5. Backhands: Swing the glove-side leg over, and receive the ball with a wide stance.

    6. Bare-handed: Skim the ground with the fingers, stay low, and be able to make one quick step before throwing.

    7. Shorthops: Field scoops and picks.

    8. Tags: Slap tags on, behind, in front, left, and right of an imaginary base.

    9. Stretch: Reach out for the toss while pushing off of an imaginary base.

    10. One-handed Flips: For double plays, toss balls straight on and to the side of your partner (older players).

    11. Blocking: Knock down a tricky bounce with the chest (nose over the ball).

    12. Quick Toss: Play quick catch with tennis balls.

    13. Line Drive: Fire balls to each other from close range.

14. *Transitions:* Pass the ball behind the back and between the legs, then switch directions.

15. *Self Pop-ups:* Toss balls into the air, and catch with two hands.

TEAM OUTFIELD DRILLS

Age: 6 years and up.

Object: Learn a series of fundamental drills to practice over and over.

Equipment: Incrediballs and gloves.

Rules: Explain and demonstrate each of the disciplines. Work in pairs or as a group. Include the following:

1. *Drop to a Knee:* Crouch down and block the ball (hard hit ground ball with no one on base).

2. *Grounders:* Receive the ball out front and pivot to throw.

3. *Circle:* Same as above except circle balls to the left and right.

4. *Shoestring:* Scoop balls hit just in front of you.

5. *Point Drill:* Use the crossover step to change directions while going back on a ball.

6. *Over the Shoulder:* Catch balls thrown directly over the head.

7. *Fence Drill:* Feel for the fence, and leap high for a ball.

8. *Self Pop-ups:* Toss balls into the air, and catch with two hands.

9. *Cutoff Drill:* Throw balls at a target on a wall or backstop.

FIELDING GAMES AND ACTIVITIES

Infield-Outfield

Age: 10 years and up.

Object: Learn a basic pre-game infield-outfield routine. Try to work in a 10-minute frame.

Equipment: Balls, bases, fungoes and gloves.

Rules: Part I: Start with the outfielders throwing twice to each base. First second base, then third, and finally home. Use cutoff people. Pitchers can field comebackers and work on covering first base. Catchers can be fielding bunts and throwing to first base as well.

Part II: Infielders should start by throwing the ball twice around the infield to each person. Then field a series of grounders. Get on the grass, and throw to home plate. Then throw twice to first base (first basemen throw to third). Work in the catchers at each stop. Next is "One and Cover" where the catcher throws to each base (make tags). Then perform two double plays each. Try a long throw from deep in your position (use the backhand). Conclude with a bare-handed toss and the catcher pop-up.

During Part II, outfielders should shag fly balls as a group in center field. The instructor should stand in foul territory with a bucket of balls. Just keep hitting them one after another. Don't use a cutoff man. After catching each variety (routine, balls left and right, over the head, line drive, and shallow pop-up), toss the ball to an open area which is in front of and away from the group.

Part III: During the final infield scenario, line everyone up down the foul line on your dugout side. Exchange glove slaps. During the entire routine, hustle and talk it up. Throw the ball hard. Hit the cutoff person. Use newer balls for a touch of class.

Four-Way Grounders

Age: 10 years and up.

Object: Use four people hitting to each of the infield positions. Cuban coaches are even known to hit fungoes *between* innings.

Equipment: Balls, fungo bats, and gloves.

Rules: Set up four people hitting to the four infield positions. Set up an equal number of balls at each spot. The first hitter to finish should yell, "Bats down!" That means everyone stops to gather the balls. After a successful fielding play, simply toss the ball behind you into the outfield. From the first base sideline, hit to the third basemen and shortstops. From the third base sideline, hit to the second and first basemen. Use extra players (pitchers or outfielders) as feeders to quicken the activity along. For multiple players at one position either take two at a time or one and out. Also, add in balls left and right, backhands, line drives, pop-ups, and actual throws, for example. Avoid chasing dribblers, or errant hits or throws.

Note: Between innings infielders should work on different fielding disciplines while receiving throws from the first baseman.

Train

Age: 10 years and up.
Object: After four-way grounders, assemble "the cutoff train" in the outfield.
Equipment: Balls, fungo bat, and gloves.
Rules: Hit fly balls from a foul line to the outfielders in center field. Have one person go at a time. The infielders should form one gigantic "train" from the outfield grass back to the person hitting. Stand in formation along the back of the infield dirt, so you're not in the "line of fire." Practice cutoffs with each toss. Remember to shade to your glove side, and make tosses to that particular area. With balls coming and going, before throwing make sure that the next person in line is looking at you.

Cutoff

Age: 9 years and up.
Object: Cutoffs can be a coach's biggest joy or most painful headache. How many times have you seen an overthrown cutoff to home plate with the hitter advancing to second base? It occurs more often than you think, even in the major leagues. This game teaches proper cutoff technique from the thrower and fielder. It's also a great throwing warm-up.
Equipment: Balls and gloves.
Rules: Have two groups of people (equal number in each). Line up down both foul lines or throughout the diamond (for more than two groups). Fielders should be an equal distance apart. Throw the ball to the cutoff person next in line as quickly and efficiently as possible. Throws begin from the home plate area, go in succession to players all the way out to the outfield fence, and then back to home plate. Fielders should have their arms up as the cutoff person, and shade their glove shoulder (quicker transfer) towards the next person in line. All players must catch (with two hands) and

throw. If a person overthrows his/her intended target, the ball must come back to that person who made the original throw and be thrown again. Use a time frame (30 to 60 seconds) to see how many successful transitions can be accomplished. Back and forth equals 1 point. Rotate people up a spot after each game. You can also try this game as a race between teams.

Relay

Age: 9 years and up.
Object: This relay race includes the cutoff play into a running game.
Equipment: Cones, balls, and fielding gloves.
Rules: Make equal teams. Place a cone and ball directly in front of each group (normal cutoff distance for age group). Teams should stand behind their own cone. At the starting signal, the first person in line runs to the cone. The next person in line throws the ball to his/her partner in pure cutoff fashion. Fielders should yell, "Hit me!" with their arms up. On a successful catch the receiver then runs with the ball back to his or her team, and puts the ball back at the front of the line. The two partners must slap gloves with one person sprinting to the cone and the other returning to the back of the line. The rotation keeps going until every person has thrown the ball at least once.

For smaller group sizes, have each person throw the ball five times. For overthrows, the person must retrieve the ball, run back and tag the cone, and only then return to the team. Add in tags (at the cone) after successful catches. Always have throws going away from the group, so errant tosses do not hit anyone else.

Pointer

Age: 9 years and up.
Object: This footwork drill simulates balls hit over an outfielder's head, to the left, and to the right. Work on being comfortable with the drop and crossover steps.
Equipment: Balls and gloves.
Rules: Have an outfielder stand ready in the fielding position. The

instructor points which way to run: back, left or right. Use the drop-step and stay low. The outfielder must run and cross over according to the direction of the "point." Don't take your eyes off of the ball. You should be on an angle to the play, never flat-footed or with your chest facing home plate. After a few "points," throw the ball so the person can catch it. Catch the easier ones with two hands. After a turn run back to the line away from the playing area. This drill can also be used for infielders going back after pop-ups.

Elway Drill

Age: 9 years and up.
Object: In honor of John Elway, a former New York Yankee draft pick out of Stanford University, this is a fun outfield drill.
Equipment: Football.
Rules: Preach that virtually every fly ball hit in the outfield should be an out. Undoubtedly this is not a true statement, but instill this attitude into the kids' minds. Arrange the group in the outfield grass. The fielder should dart off into the distance with the instructor lofting the football in his/her direction. Diving is highly encouraged. First, work on easy catches with short routes. Second, work on difficult catches with long routes. Third, run patterns left and right. Fourth, run after the ball thrown directly over the head.

Green Monster

Age: 9 years and up.
Object: In honor of the left field wall at Fenway Park, this competitive outfield game combines aggressiveness, communication, and the clutch catch.
Equipment: Cones, balls, gloves and fence.
Rules: Align two teams

on each side of the outfield or foul fences. Use cones to establish out of bounds on both sides. Players should throw the ball back and forth over the fence. Any ball hitting the ground becomes a point for the throwing team. Fielders need to communicate upon catching the ball. Play to a set score, or use a series format.

Qué Pasa?

Age: 9 years and up.

Object: "Qué Pasa?" is Spanish for "what's up?" This activity simulates game situations and visualizing one's job in the field and on the bases.

Equipment: Balls, bat, gloves, helmets and bases.

Rules: Arrange a fielding team and a baserunning team. The instructor hits from home plate. Runners (with helmets) start from a boundary (use a cone or helmet) away from home plate. Runners can only advance after contact is made. Pitchers can either make an actual or simulated throw to the catcher. Include base coaches. Play "situations" such as base hits, fly balls, pop-ups, ground balls, bunts, cutoffs, relay throws, backing up, sliding, and even the infield-fly rule. After three outs, clear the bases. After six outs, the base runners should become fielders.

Each player has a role: fielder, base runner, or base coach. All fielders should yell out the number of outs after each is recorded. Runners should show the number of outs with their finger(s). The instructor should also take pitches to see if infielders and outfielders are moving with the pitch, or covering bases on bunt situations. A competitive game can also be devised to see which team scores the most runs. For older kids, incorporate more advanced plays such as bunt coverage, double cutoffs, or double plays. No matter what the age level, explain both mistakes and positive plays.

Mini Di

Age: 9 years and up.

Object: Create a small field with bases about 20 to 30 feet apart as a way to explain strategy and certain game situations.

Equipment: Bases, balls and gloves.

Rules: Have nine players take the field with everyone else watching. Rotate each player into the field after five plays; use base runners at a later juncture. The instructor (throw the ball where you want it to go) can mimic bunt coverage, duties for backing up, cutoffs, double plays, on-deck batter responsibilities, rundowns, pop-ups, offensive signals, first-and-third offense and defense, pickoffs, and pitchouts (the latter four: high school and up). This activity is best served just before the start of a season. The main reason for the short field is so everyone can easily hear the instructor talking.

                                      —Leigh Hogan.

Fielding Relays

Age: 8 years and up.
Object: Teach fielding techniques in a group activity.
Equipment: Balls and gloves.
Rules: Have the infielders work in the infield and the outfielders in the outfield. Set up third basemen and shortstops on the left side of the infield. Have the second and first basemen work on the right side. The fielders should face each other. One person with a ball rolls it to the person in the other line. After a throw sprint to the other line. Fielders should work on the receiving stance, circling and charging the ball, and a smooth transfer. For outfielders, set up two groups in left field and another in right field. Toss fly balls to each other. After a throw run to the other line. Always circle the ball and catch with two hands. This becomes a nice conditioning exercise.

Mission Impossible

Age: 10 years and up.
Object: Preach an aggressive defensive philosophy.
Equipment: Tennis balls, gloves, and fungo bats.
Rules: One player stands in the fielding position just away from a wall. Four or five people, standing together, at the same time each hit a ground ball in the direction of a fielder. This person has

to make as many catches as possible. Award two points for clean catches, and one point for keeping the ball in front of them. How many balls can one field, catch, or block in a single turn?

Last Man

Age: 9 years and up.
Object: The goal here is to react and somehow catch a line drive.
Equipment: Incrediballs, fungo bat, and gloves.
Rules: Explain a balanced fielding position and the importance of a quick first step. Make a line of fielders with one person going at a single time. The instructor hits a line drive (ground ball or in the air) at the fielder. That person (vary for skill level) must make a clean catch. No bobbles or drops are allowed. Compensate for base hits. If successful you get to stay in line. Progress to liners in different directions. The winner ("last man standing") should receive a group applause.

Goalie

Age: 9 years and up.
Object: Ice hockey goalies need lightning-quick reflexes. This game serves notice that kids need a good jump on the ball, and to always keep it in front of them.
Equipment: Bats, Incrediballs and gloves.
Rules: Depending on space behind the backstop or soccer net, place one team on either side. Hit ground balls to one fielder standing in the middle of the backstop. The fielder must make a clean catch or block it with their body (nose over ball) to keep the ball from going into the rectangular frame area. The target adds to the difficulty and intrigue of this game. For competitive purposes,

increase the target distance (larger fielding area), velocity of the ground balls, perfect catches (no bobbles), add in a throw back to an instructor (or another player), or scores between teams. The winners from each side can play a championship round. When indoors tape a target area on the wall.

You-Me

Age: 6 years and up.
Object: In order to teach priorities in the outfield, try the "You-Me" activity.
Equipment: Bat, gloves and balls.
Rules: Indoors or outside, arrange outfielders in pairs or in an actual game day alignment. First, hit ground balls into the gaps, so the outfielders have to verbally communicate either "you" or "me" as to priority on the catch. Encourage hustle and backing up. Remember to circle the ball. Second, hit line drives to the gaps. Third, hit fly balls over their heads. Fourth, hit fly balls to the fences so their backs are to the play. Whoever does *not* field the ball should be watching the advancing base runner, and communicate the proper cutoff message to their teammate. Proper communication in the outfield adds to outs and subtracts from collision injuries.

Back-Up

Age: 9 years and up.
Object: Missing a back-up duty in a game can cost a team a win. Stress the importance of backing up in a practice activity.
Equipment: Bat, gloves and balls.
Rules: Arrange a fielding lineup. Hit fly balls and grounders. On each ball hit, every player should be doing something. Whether it's pitchers backing up the plate on throws home, catchers running behind first base on ground balls in the infield, outfielders backing each other up on fly balls, or middle infielders backing up throws to the pitcher with a runner on third base—pre-think your role on each situation. Incorporate double cutoffs and run-scoring base hits. Extra players can run the bases (wear helmets).

Tip: In order to be in the proper position, always expect a fielding error or an overthrow on every play. The coach should also remember to recite the ground rules before each game.

P.F.P.

Age: 13 years and up.

Object: Incorporate "P.F.P." (Pitcher's Fielding Practice) into one 10-to-15 minute session.

Equipment: Bases, gloves and balls.

Rules: In each drill make a simulated pitch home. When hitting comebackers, people next in line should stand away from the mound. Preach a good fielding position after release, cat-like reflexes, getting a good grip on the ball, and a complete follow through. Remember, you're the fifth infielder out there!

1. Right Side: Arrange all of the pitchers on the mound. From home plate hit balls to the first baseman. The pitcher must sprint to and up the foul line, give a glove target to the first baseman, catch the toss, tag the bag, and turn to look for another play. The catcher should yell, "Get over there!" Try 3 to 5 apiece.

2. Comebackers: Hit ground balls back to the mound. The pitcher should field/block the ball and throw to first base (never bare hand it). After the catch, the catcher should yell, "Step and throw!" to the pitcher. Do five apiece.

3. Bunts: Have three lines of pitchers and three catchers (rolling out bunts). The bunt should reflect the toss according to first, second, or third base. Angle the body properly according to a left- or right-handed thrower, so you do not have to spin around. Do each discipline three times.

4. Double Plays: Hit ground balls back towards the mound simulating a bases-loaded, no-out situation. The pitcher should field the ball, and throw a strike to the catcher. Next, field the ball for a throw to second base. Square up and shuffle the feet until you're in a good throwing position. Always follow your throw. Do each discipline twice. In the event of a bobble or late/non-call, the pitcher should get the out at first base.

5. *Pickoffs* (baseball): Explain the specific type of pickoff according to each base. Specify whether the pitchers pivot on their own move or from the infielder's signal. Have three lines near the mound throwing to either first, second, or third base. Perform each task three times. The middle line, throwing off of the rubber, throws to second base. The left line (only right-handers) should perform a pickoff to third base. The right line should do a pickoff to first. Pitchers can also play catch with each other in a group while performing the step-off or spin-move styles of pickoffs.

—Eddie Riley.

I Got It

Age: All.

Object: Practicing pop-ups and fly balls should be a part of every practice.

Equipment: Gloves and balls.

Rules: Spread fielders apart (infielders, outfielders, catchers) in various spots on the field or in the gymnasium. Teach the proper technique of catching the ball with two hands, above the head, and over the throwing shoulder. Then have the kids catch 50 pop-ups by throwing the ball to themselves. Verbally call for the ball on each catch. Teach them how to catch a "sun ball" (use the gym lights) by blocking the glare with their glove. The more space you have, the more difficult the catches can be (i.e. in front, back, left or right).

When doing situational plays outdoors, issue fielding priorities according to their numbered positions. Except for right field (9) over center (8), the higher number has priority. For example: Center fielder (8) over the shortstop (6), or first baseman (3) over the catcher (2). Try calling for the ball by actually yelling out your position number. *Note:* Beginning players can perform this drill with a foam or rag ball.

Super Catch

Age: 8 years and up.
Object: Add some creativity to catching routine fly balls.
Equipment: Incrediballs and gloves.
Rules: Partner up. Throw high fly balls to each other. No running catches are allowed. Each person must catch the fly some way other than normal.

—Mike Andrews Baseball Camp.

Around the Horn

Age: 9 years and up.
Object: This game manifests zipping the ball around the infield. Whether on force outs, steal plays, or after a strikeout infielders should be accustomed to throwing to every base.
Equipment: Four bases, gloves and balls.
Rules: Place infielders at each bag (straddle) on the actual diamond plus the catcher in front of home plate. Rotate the direction of the throws after each completed round. First, go catcher to third to second to first to catcher. Second, go catcher to first to shortstop to third to catcher. After a successful round, add in tag plays. Back-ups should jump into the action after each throw. Communication can also be added with a fielder yelling out the bag he/she is going to throw to. Most teams use this exercise as part of their pre-game infield practice. After a strikeout in a regular game, the catcher should throw to third base (against left-handed batters) and to first base (against right-handed batters).

King Cone

Age: 7 to 11 years old.
Object: This is a fun game where kids learn about throwing and catching. A regulation ball adds an element of the tag play.

Equipment: Four bases, four cones, and soccer ball (bat, gloves, and regulation ball are optional).

Rules: Make two teams. Place a cone on the outside corner of each base including one on top of home plate. Put a fielder at each base (total of three) along with a pitcher and catcher. Everyone else stands wherever they want. The hitting team has one kicker at a time. A soccer ball is rolled at the cone near home plate. After a kick this person sprints around the bases. While this is going on, the ball must be retrieved and passed successfully to the people at first, second, third, and then home. After each catch, the fielder must knock down his/her cone before throwing to the next base.

Outs include the following: 1) A pitched ball which hits the cone at home plate, 2) a ball caught in the air by a fielder, 3) the batter knocking down a cone, or 4) two foul balls in a row. A run is scored if the batter reaches home plate before the ball gets there. Play three outs per inning, or have each player on a team get a turn at bat. For older kids, use a bat, regulation ball, and gloves. After a hit, the ball must be thrown around the infield in similar fashion. This time, after a catch the fielder must knock the cone over as in a tag play.

—Assumption College Sports Camp.

Box Drill

Age: 10 years and up.
Object: This drill works on the quick pivot, double-play transition, and getting the ball out of the glove quickly.
Equipment: Four bases, tennis balls (gloves and regulation balls optional), and a whistle.

Rules: Separate players into groups of four in the shape of a box (minia-
ture diamond). Extra players can rotate into the action after a throw.
Large teams can assemble make-shift diamonds in the outfield as
well. Arrange fielders according to their positions. Instruct players
to straddle the bag, keep their feet moving, receive a throw with
the hands out front ("open glove"), make a quick transfer, and
release the ball out front.

First, start with easy tosses to each corner. Focus on catching
the ball and then making a good throw. Middle infielders should
be hopping after a throw (simulating a sliding base runner). Second, throw in the opposite direction. Stress the quick pivot, and
getting the body in a balanced throwing position and square to the
throwing target. Use a whistle to switch directions. Third, add
gloves and regular balls, and increase the distances. Tag plays can
also be incorporated. Fourth, use a competitive atmosphere for
older players where the infield group has to make perfect catches
and tosses (no bobbles or misses) for one straight minute. Keep
going until they accomplish the goal. Also, see which group can
make the most relay throws in a certain time period (four touches
equals one point).

Orbit

Age: 9 years and up.
Object: Similar to the Earth rotating around the sun, infielders should
practice fielding quickly and accurately from side to side. The focus
for this activity is for improved hand-eye coordination, catching
with two hands, and a quick transfer.
Equipment: Balls, gloves, and a whistle.
Rules: Arrange the group in a large circle. Pass a ball left to right and
then right to left. Use a whistle to switch directions. Then add in
more than one ball. For individual work, quickly pass the ball
between your legs (both sides) and behind your back. Try not to
drop the ball. Get the proper grip each time. Attempt this bare-
handed and then with gloves.
> —Mike O'Brien.

Have a Ball

Age: 8 years and up.

Object: This fielding activity sharpens hand-eye coordination and reaction time. It's also great as a warm-up drill.

Equipment: 20 balls for each pair of teammates.

Rules: Two players should stand 8 to 10 feet apart with the first kneeling and the other crouched over as if fielding a ground ball. Player 1 should have all of the balls in front of him/her. Player 1 tosses all 20 balls to Player 2—one at a time and as fast as possible. Player 2 aims to catch or bat down every ball with alternating hands. When the balls run out the players should switch positions. Each player should field 20 balls.

　　　　　　　　—Rules: Kellogg's *Earn Your Stripes*
　　　　　　　　Baseball Drills Series.

Bone Rack

Age: 7 years and up.

Object: This elimination game stresses proper fielding technique and quick, clean throws.

Equipment: Bats, balls, bases, gloves and helmets.

Rules: A mythic tribal ritual says that cavemen were thrown bones of saber-toothed tigers. One had to catch or block the bone, and then throw it to the head of the family. The person to catch or block the most bones would then be anointed the "Bone Rack King or Queen."

　　　For "Infielder Bone Rack," line the kids up behind shortstop (older kids) or second base. Hit a ground ball to them. That person must either make a clean catch, keep it in front or 1 to 2 feet behind, and then make a good throw (depending on skill level) to someone standing at first base. That catch, even on a scoop, jump or lunge, must keep the receiver on the base for the fielder to continue on in the game. After an error, however, all players recite the famous Arnold Schwarzenegger line, "Hasta la vista, baby." Those eliminated must report to the "Bone Rack Den" near the third base dugout area (form a circle with the helmets). A fielder is also eliminated if they pick the ball up with their glove instead of the bare hand. For older players, the catch and throw cannot have any bobbles or miscues. To increase the level of difficulty, add in harder hit balls.

For "Outfielder Bone Rack," players need to make clean catches of fly balls hit from the instructor. Any drop eliminates that fielder (see rules above) from the game. Add in accurate cutoff throws as well. The "Bone Rack King or Queen" (last person standing) can be awarded a Burger King crown.

          —Dave Smith and Bob Casaceli.

Seven Hundred Club

Age: 6 years and up.
Object: This game can be played anywhere with any number of kids.
Equipment: Bat, balls and gloves.
Rules: Start with one batter and everyone else as the fielders some distance away. Fielders can stand anywhere they want. The batter throws the ball up in the air and hits it out into the field or gym. Points are awarded to the person who catches the ball. There are also fielding deductions for errors. Scoring includes: A diving catch (200 points), routine fly ball catch (100), ground ball catch which bounces once (75), ground ball catch which bounces twice (50), and any ground ball catch which bounces more than twice (25).

    Deductions due to fumbling, misses, or drops include: ball skipping past you (minus 200 points), fly ball error (minus 100), ground ball error which bounces once (minus 75), ground ball error which bounces twice (minus 50), and any ground ball error which bounces more than twice (minus 25). After every catch a score should be called out loud. Once a fielder scores 700 points, that person switches places with the hitter. Upon a fielder-hitter switch, all scores return to zero. Players should keep track of their own scores. You can also use a live pitcher in this game.

Anything Goes

Age: 9 years and up.
Object: Teach strategy and risk on behalf of the defense.
Equipment: Anything used for a regular game.

Rules: Divide players up equally. The defensive team can play any-where. For example: Play a hitter to pull or to the opposite field,  in for slap hitters, or behind the outfield fence to steal a home run. There are no base runners (instruc-tor's discretion). Hitters get a 1-and-1 count (use strikeouts and walks). After a walk, the hitter has the option of staying with that result and/or stay-ing up with a new count (also applies for a hit by pitch). Base hits include: single (any-thing landing in the outfield grass or via fielding error), double (ball rolling to the fence), triple (hitting fence in the air), and home run (landing over fence without being caught). Fielders should hustle to halt balls from reaching the fence. Runs are scored in traditional fashion: bases-loaded hit scores one, etc. No bunting or sacrifice flies. Fielders can also earn points (runs) through exemplary catches. There are no limits to defensive runs. Play different posi-tions each inning.

You Field It

Age: 10 years and up.

Object: This is a fielding and hitting game with points for catches and base hits.

Equipment: Equipment used in on-field batting practice.

Rules: Set up a pitching screen with a bucket of baseballs. Have a coach pitch. Place a fielder at the seven positions (no catcher). There are offensive and defensive points to be made. A successful catch (ground ball or fly ball) is one point. A missed or dropped catch is a point for the batter and a minus point for that particular fielder. Hitters get points for base hits, and bonus points for extra base hits. Thus, this game is live action. For example, a ground ball to shortstop and subsequent clean catch is a point for the fielder and also the hitter. A double to the right field fence is two points for the batter and zero points for the right fielder. Try one fair ball hit, or three fair ball hits per batter. But batters should stay up until they hit a fair ball unless a foul ball is caught in the air. Rotate positions after every hitter (first-to-second, second-to-third, third-to-shortstop, shortstop-to-left field, left field-to-center, and right field-to-on-deck). You can have more than one on-deck batter. Each batter should be allowed an equal number of chances to hit. Kids can keep track of their individual scores.

—Dave Smith.

Dump

Age: 9 years and up.

Object: The success of a defensive team all depends on the ability to successfully field grounders or fly balls.

Equipment: Four helmets, four bats, gloves and balls.

Rules: Make two teams with an equal number of strong/weak fielders on both sides. Put a team at shortstop and another at second base. Place a helmet beside each group. Two instructors (each side of home plate) hit to the different lines. The number of balls in a group must equal the number of kids in a line. For safety reasons have the fielders stand away from the rest of the group. At the starting signal, the instructors hit to the first people in line. After successfully fielding the grounder, that person runs to his/her team's helmet and puts the ball inside. Once this occurs, the instructors can hit to the next person in that line. Thus, hitting will typically be occurring at different times.

If a grounder is missed that person has to run and get the ball, and put it in the helmet. After a successful turn go to the end of the line. Also, if a ball falls out of the helmet the hitter cannot continue until all balls are back in. If a teammate stops a ball from going into the outfield, a "Benny Bombington" shall be called. The instructor should ask for the ball, and hit/throw a "bomb" far into the outfield. That subsequent fielder must then return the ball back to the helmet before the rotation can continue.

After all of the balls are in the helmet, the instructor should yell, "Dump." The last person to field a ball has to run with the helmet full of balls to his/her instructor, and dump the balls inside a designated circle or area. That kid then returns the helmet to their line, gets back in line, and hitting continues. After five "dumps" (the team counts out loud after the completion of each one) the game is over. Use a colored ball as the final "dump ball."

For "Outfielder Dump," use similar rules as above with one exception: any fly ball or pop-up not caught must be either thrown or run back to the person hitting. Thus, all balls placed in the helmet must first be caught cleanly.

       —Dave Smith and Bob Casaceli.

Shadow Ball

Age: 10 years and up.

Object: Back in the Negro Leagues, players would sometimes go through their fielding and cutoff drills *without* a ball. They were so convincing that many fans thought that what they saw was indeed real.

Equipment: Bats and gloves.

Rules: Arrange the group in a pre-game infield/outfield routine. Yell out instructions for each phase: infield, outfield, and catchers included. Start with a simulated swing to left field, then center field, and so on. Encourage the kids to dive, yell out cutoff instructions, back up bases, and zip the "ball" to their teammates with authority and intensity. Slap the glove with your hand to make it sound like a catch. Bang two bats together to simulate contact. Make it as real as possible. This can be a great way to end practice as well as teaching fielding position and techniques. Those daring enough could even try this as a motivational ploy just before a game.

Juggling

Age: 10 years and up.

Object: Juggling is the ultimate in hand-eye coordination. It takes a keen eye and hand to keep the balls in the air for an extended period.

Equipment: Tennis balls or bean bags.

Rules: Start by tossing one ball in the air with your dominant hand (hold it in your fingertips). Catch it with your other hand. Repeat this over and over. Now reverse the direction of the ball with your non-dominant hand. Repeat this over and over. Then put a ball in each hand, and toss the ball from your dominant hand towards your other hand. When this ball reaches the top of its arc, toss the ball from your other hand towards your dominant hand (below the arc of the first ball). Catch the balls and repeat it over and over. Now reverse the direction of the balls, non-dominant hand first. Talk to yourself and get a rhythm by saying, "One, two, one, two." Don't get frustrated. Juggling isn't easy but keep trying. Try it as a competition or an activity during a break in the action.

Flip

Age: 9 years and up.

Object: This is a fun game of catching the ball and flipping it to a teammate. Take a page out of the old "Gas House Gang." The likes of Pepper Martin, Enos Slaughter, Leo Durocher,  and Frankie Frisch would juggle the ball, bounce it off of their chests, flick it off of their gloves, pass it between their legs, kick it off of their cleats, roll it down their arms, and fake their throws with the ball going in a different direction. It was amazing what they could do with the ball, and you should have seen them play!

Equipment: Gloves and a ball; Incrediball for younger kids.

Rules: Make a circle with about 10 people. Start by flipping the ball to someone else in the circle. The receiver can use any part of his/her body to keep the ball in the air, but can only pass the ball from out of the glove. No bare-handed tosses. Advanced players can try to fake out a teammate.

Players must turn their hat to one side if they 1) make a poor toss, 2) make an error, or 3) drop the ball. If a hat makes a complete circle (side right, back, left, and then front) that person has to do 10 push-ups. To really test for "soft hands" bring in a carton of eggs. Toss them back and forth (no gloves). The fielder wants to give with their hands, and to cradle the egg by bringing the top hand over the bottom. Bean bags or small water balloons can be used as substitutes. Keep increasing the distances between the partners after each successful catch. *Tip:* Infielders should own small gloves and break them in (circular shape), so the ball can exit the mitt in the quickest possible fashion. No glove should ever look like a pancake.

Bat Flip

Age: 14 years and up.

Object: This activity challenges the group to bounce a ball in the air, from bat to bat, as many times as possible. This game is similar to "Flip" except you're using bats instead of gloves.

Equipment: Bats and balls.

Rules: Make a circle of players each equipped with a bat. One person lobs the ball to someone else in the circle. That person tries to hit the ball in the air to another person and so on. Count how many times the group can successfully keep the ball in the air without it hitting the ground—using only a bat. The ball hitting the same person's bat more than once in a single turn only counts as one point towards the total. Keep a running tally of the high score during the season.

Two Ball

Age: 10 years and up.
Object: This is a terrific pre-game activity.
Equipment: Two balls.
Rules: Circle up. One person should start with two balls in one hand. Toss the two balls at the same time to someone else in the group. The balls must be flipped, not thrown on a line, within the vicinity of this person's spot in the circle. Don't make the arc too high. The receiver must try and catch both balls with their hands. You can't use your chest. If either ball drops to the ground, this person must turn his/her hat to the side. For subsequent drops the hat should turn back, to the side, front, etc.

After a full turn, that person is eliminated from the group. The last person remaining wins. If you catch both balls with one hand, you have the option of reducing one turn of your own hat or adding a turn to the person who tossed you the balls. For a large group playing "Two Ball," make the latter an elimination factor; plus, you're also eliminated if any toss hits the ground first.
—Lowell American Legion Baseball Team.

One Toss

Age: 12 years and up.
Object: To remain the last player standing by not dropping the tossed ball.
Equipment: Baseballs.
Rules: Start with a circle of players each with a ball in one hand. Someone starts the game by tossing the "game ball" into play. As soon as a player catches that ball he/she fires the next one off. Aim for a high intensity fast-moving game. Deceptive throws include the no-look, the behind-the-back, and the high-low—anything to confuse the person who's receiving your toss. After three drops or misses, a person is eliminated from the game with the circle getting smaller and smaller until two people are left. This game is a combination of pin-ball, shadow ball, juggling and flip. Watch a

crew of college players powering out this game, and you'll most
certainly see some entertainment unfold.
                    —Wareham Gatemen.

Knockout

Age: 6 years and up.
Object: This game combines fielding technique with throwing on the run.
Equipment: Incrediball or tennis ball, and gloves (optional).
Rules: Field with or without gloves. Form one long line of kids behind
a marker. Start by throwing the ball against a cement wall (indoors
or outside). After a toss, hustle to the back of the line. The next
person must then field the ball, throw it, return to the end of the
line, and so on.

Throws must be hard. No one can shield a fielder from the ball.
Anyone who makes an error (apply to skill skills) or hits the ground
with a throw is eliminated from the competition. Also, catching a
ball off of the wall in the air eliminates that particular thrower.
Alternate the variations. First, two-handed catches and throws.
Second, charging hard and throwing on-the-run.
                    —Rich Gedman Baseball Camp.

Stoopball

Age: 7 years and up.
Object: To develop speed and accurracy.
Equipment: A ball with bounce.
Rules: "Stoopball is played in the street in front of a building with
steps with 2 to 3 people per team. One team is in the field and the
other at bat. The batter faces the building and throws the ball at
the steps as hard as he/she can. The ball must hit the steps and
bounce back into the street. The batter is out if someone in the field
catches the ball on a fly. If not, it is a hit. The number of bases the
ghost runners advance is determined by the number of times the
ball bounces before it is caught (1 bounce=single, 2 bounces=dou-
ble, 3 bounces=triple, 4 or more bounces=home run). Also, one
bobble by the fielder is a single. If the ball gets by a fielder

untouched it's double. If the ball goes over a fielder's head it's a home run. Runs are scored just as in baseball. Three outs per team. Play seven or nine innings."

—Spaldeen Games, www.spaldeen.com.

Copy Cat

Age: 6 years and up.
Object: This is a competitive game between two or more fielders.
Equipment: Ball and gloves (optional).
Rules: Start the game by throwing a ball against the wall. Then do something before you catch it. The next person has to do exactly the same thing. For example: Throw and catch the ball after one bounce. Throw and catch with a spin, clap, or without moving the feet. Throw with the eyes shielded, or catch with the bare hand. Throw and catch with a push-up or sit-up. Try clicking the heels. Avoid repeating the same play twice. Use a marker for the starting line. Try "Copy Cat" as an elimination game, or a friendly competition.

—Rich Gedman Baseball Camp.

La Boca

Age: All.
Object: La boca is Spanish for "the mouth." Teams need fielders who take charge by calling out pop-ups and fly balls. Any such call should be yelled so loud that people in the next town can hear them.
Equipment: Balls and gloves.
Rules: Arrange the group in a circle, and give each person a number. Have the kids standing, kneeling, sitting, lying down, or with their eyes closed. The instructor should throw a ball high in the air from the middle of the circle and then call out a number. The person with that number should sprint to the ball, call it up, and try to make the catch. Use two hands. For youngsters who need to release some tension, declare a winner for the loudest scream.

Air Raid

Age: 11 years and up.
Object: Learn the art of the pop-up and proper communication.
Equipment: Bat, gloves and balls.
Rules: Instruct players to take their positions, and be ready for a fair
   or foul pop-up. Hit pop-ups to all nine areas of the field (remaining position players should take a knee while away from the action).
   Once a ball is in the air, everyone should be moving. Take charge
   by yelling, "Ball!" Players close to the area of the pop-up should
   be yelling, "Take it!" so the person catching the ball knows it's
   his/her job to make the catch.

   Be sure to yell out any hazards such as the actual pitching mound,
   fences, the backstop, or dugouts. Reiterate priorities: center fielder
   over other outfielders, outfielder over infielder, shortstop over any
   infielder, second baseman over first baseman, infielder over catcher
   or pitcher, and catcher over pitcher.

   Pitchers should call up pop-ups near the mound. They should
   also point and yell where the pop-up is located in order to assist
   the fielders. Players not involved in the play should be backing up
   or covering the bases. If a pop-up drops in, instructors can add in
   push-ups or sit-ups. Remember that once a pop-up is in the air
   someone should have yelled, "Up!" Once the ball has begun its
   descent to the ground, someone should have called for it. Once priority has been established then people should be communicating
   with commands or first names; the louder the better.

   End with a rapid-fire pop-up session (for older players). Have a
   bucket of balls and just keep hitting them. Everyone is eligible to
   make the catch. It's literally an "air raid" of balls. Be sure to hit
   balls to different areas (not the same place), so kids aren't running
   into each other.

Mafisto

Age: 9 years and up.
Object: This game is for the better skilled players who love to get their
   uniforms dirty.

Equipment: Incrediballs and gloves.

Rules: Tell the kids about the "legend" of former Yankee minor leaguer Bill Mafisto, who became famous for his diving catches in the 1950s. The player should make a full sprint under a long toss from an instructor. Look to make the shoestring catch, pick, scoop, over-the-shoulder, *snow cone*, or the full-body extension grab. When a player makes a tremendous snatch, together the group yells, "Mafisto!" If a player slows up to dive, the group yells, "Pseudo!" (for a lackluster attempt). You can also add in a point system: clean catches (2 points), outstretched catches (3 points), shoestring or over-the-shoulder (5 points), or that unbelievable "Mafisto" catch (10 points).

—Dave Smith and Bob Casaceli.

Superman

Age: 10 years and up.

Object: For those who like to get "air under their wings," set up a fielding game where the dive is encouraged.

Equipment: Large gymnastic mats (used for the pole vault), gloves and Incrediballs.

Rules: Each fielder should get a running start and aim to land on the large, puffy gymnastic mats. Instructors should yell, "Go!" and loft the ball towards the mat(s). Extend the body with an open glove, close it upon catching the ball, propel the body up (on ground balls) after landing, and show the umpire a catch after hitting the ground. This game is also great for the pool (no gloves).

Ultimate Pickle

Age: 9 years and up.
Object: Practice the art of the rundown.
Equipment: Numerous cones, gloves, and an Incrediball or RIF ball.
Rules: Start with a basic explanation of the rundown. Make groups of three, so each kid can field and run. Large teams can form four rundown stations in the infield plus multiple stations in the outfield. Then form two separate lines of players. Put one person in the middle serving as the runner. The runner starts with about 15 to 20 yards of space between each fielder. One fielder (with the ball) charges after the runner. Hold the ball up and in your hand. Only make one fake (wrist snap) before throwing.

Instruct the fielders to set up either left or right (inside versus outside) of the runner. Never throw a ball over the runner's head. The player receiving the ball should yell, "Now!" when he/she feels the best time to call for it. Once releasing the ball, the thrower should follow his/her throw by going to the end of the line to which the ball was thrown to. Attempt to make no more than 3 to 4 throws (depending on skill levels).

Enthusiastic runners can make this an exciting game through hustle and body fakes. If successful in making it to the end of one line, the runner can go again. The tagger becomes the next runner. Simply exchange fielding gloves with someone else to quicken the game along. Remember, a fielder cannot make any contact with the runner.

Another way to play (younger kids) is to have each fielder at a cone. Increase the distance between cones to better distinguish specific areas. A runner starts near the middle of the line. An instructor should throw the ball to a fielder closest to the runner. The runner then goes in whatever direction he/she wants. Fielders can only throw from their designated cone. Throws should be

made to the person closest to the runner. Make throws to the opposite side of the runner. If a runner makes it to the end of one line,
the defense has to do 10 push-ups.

Crash Dummy

Age: 10 years and up.
Object: Make fielders confident in approaching fences both in the
infield and outfield.
Equipment: Balls, gloves, and large gymnastic mats.
Rules: First teach the proper fielding technique for approaching a
fence. While in pursuit feel for the fence with the throwing hand,
and hoist yourself up for that highlight catch. Listen to your teammates plus the gravel of the warning track (outfielders). The
instructor should toss the balls and vary the running distances.
First, make the catches easy so kids get comfortable going back
on balls. Second, make them more difficult. Third, start scaling
the walls. While indoors players can leap up against the pushed-
in bleachers. For protection cover the fence or bleacher with gym
mats.

Mosquito

Age: 7 years and up.
Object: Practice tags as if you're slapping at a pesky mosquito.
Equipment: Actual bases or throw-down bases, balls and gloves.
Rules: Demonstrate how to properly tag a base runner and to shift
around the bag on a poor throw. Pair kids up directly in line with
each other. Use an actual base or dirt square as a target. Work on
simple tags on easy tosses. Then quicken the tosses, add in short
hops, high throws, and even throws which take the fielder to
different areas of the base: left, right, in front, or behind the bag.
For competitive purposes, work on throws and tags between partners. With each successful phase (catch and tag), increase the distances between players. If one player misses a throw or drops the
ball, that group sits down. To keep more people in the game, instead
have them do 10 push-ups or sit-ups.

Kick Softball

Age: 6 to 8 years old.

Object: Teach toddlers about positioning, backing up, and some basic rules of the game.

Equipment: Bases and soccer ball.

Rules: Make a hitting and fielding team. Apply the same rules as in softball. Draw a three-foot square in the dirt around home plate. A strike is a ball which rolls over this area, and a ball is for anything outside. Have the pitcher roll the ball to the batter at moderate speed. After a fair ball kick, the batter runs to first base. No leading or base stealing. You can also try kicking a stationary ball.

> —Victor P. Dauer and Robert P. Pangrazi, *Dynamic Physical Education for Elementary School Children*, 6th ed. (Minneapolis: Burgess Publishing Company, 1979).

Treasure Hunt

Age: All.

Object: Not a true fielding game by definition, but someone has to find all of the balls lost in the woods.

Equipment: Hopefully you find something.

Rules: After the last station on the final day of camp, for example, gather everyone in the group for a "Treasure Hunt." Start the task after all of the visible equipment is picked up and put away. The goal is to find balls, bats, helmets—anything stuck in the backstop, hidden in the woods, lurking along the fences, or nestled in the tall grass. Watch out for those picker bushes, and stay away from the poison ivy. Give out bubble gum or baseball cards to those who find the most equipment.

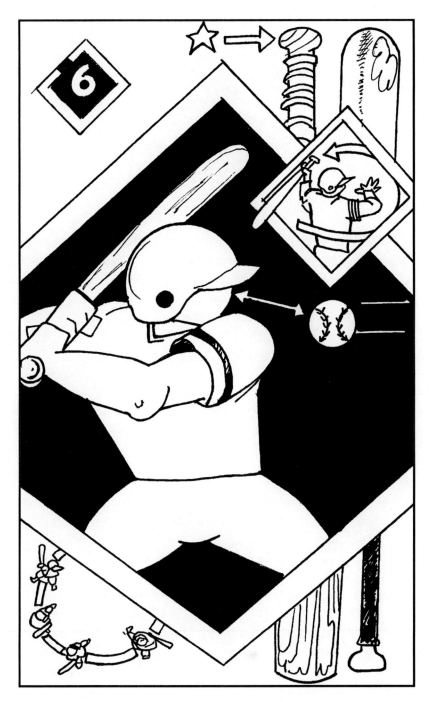

Hitting

I believe the youth idea is great with some minor leagues: Put an eight-foot board fence around the playing area and only let the kids inside; take away all uniforms and let the kids wear street clothes; let them choose teams by the one potato, two potato system; let them play until it gets dark or until the kid with the ball goes home.—*David Gey*

The Basics

Bat and Grip: First select a bat which is right for you; light enough to control yet heavy enough for a hard swing. Gently grip it at the knob with both hands. Hold the bat with the fingers, not the palms.

Stance: Stand straight up in the batter's box and face home plate. Be balanced with the feet wider than shoulder's width apart. The front foot should be placed near the plate's midpoint. Bend the knees, lean over slightly, and turn the head to face the pitcher. Put the hands near the back shoulder with the bat behind the head. The rear arm should be level or relaxed while the front arm is shaped like the letter "L." Tilt the front shoulder down slightly. Focus on the ball as it's released from the pitcher. Start with most of the weight on the back leg.

Stride: As the pitch is coming, cock the hands back and rotate the front shoulder in slightly. Take a small step forward. Place the front foot down on the big toe.

Swing: The basic two-handed swing is a powerful yet fluid movement. While starting the hips towards the pitcher, shift the weight from the back leg to the front leg. Direct the bat straight down to the ball. Extend the arms, and forcefully swing at strikes located from the knees to the middle of the chest.

Aim to make contact in front of home plate. The bat should be almost level on contact with a firm front leg (foot pointing at the plate) and bent back leg (heel off ground). The hips should rotate around with the bellybutton facing the pitcher. Keep the head still, and both eyes fixated on the ball throughout the swing. Instead of guessing, react to the location of the pitch.

Follow Through: After contact, the top-hand wrist turns over the bottom. Allow the bat to come completely around and hit the backside. The batter should be balanced straight up and down. After hitting the ball, drop the bat near the plate and sprint towards first base. In normal situations concentrate on making contact and hitting the ball hard. Progress to hitting inside pitches to the pull side and outside pitches to the opposite field.

TEAM HITTING DRILLS

Age: All (specifics depend upon skill levels).

Object: As an all-inclusive swinging drill, place the hitters in a circle or in lines. Leave plenty of space between people. Here the swing is broken down into separate components.

Equipment: Bats for everyone. Use old hockey sticks as extra "bats" for large groups. Put a cap down for home plate.

Rules: Slowly demonstrate the five parts of the swing; one at a time, leading up to one complete, balanced, and aggressive swing. Use verbal commands for each phase.

    1. Movement: Have movement with the bat and "happy feet" while in the stance. Stand relaxed and balanced with the weight back.

    2. Stride: Use a "soft stride" directly towards the pitcher. Keep the hands up and the weight back.

    3. Cock: Get the hands moving just before the pitch. After the stride, jerk the hands back and the front shoulder in slightly. Don't move the head.

    4. Contact: Together shift the weight to the front leg, and forcefully thrust the hands on a direct line towards the pitch. Extend the arms. Hit the ball just in front of home plate.

    5. Follow Through: After contact swing the bat up and around the head. Let it hit the backside.

HITTING GAMES AND ACTIVITIES

Magician

Age: 13 years and up.

Object: Learn how to release the top hand off of the bat after contact.

Hit just like Ken Griffey, Jr., Tony Gwynn, and Bernie Williams. This is another all-inclusive drill, and could be done directly following "Team Hitting." This type of swing looks like a magician who's trying some hocus-pocus.

Equipment: Bats for each person. Use old hockey sticks as extra "bats" for large groups. Put a cap down for home plate.

Rules: Arrange the batters in a circle or in lines. Use verbal commands for each phase. This swing is broken down into five separate parts.

1. *Movement:* Have movement with the bat and "happy feet" while in the stance. Stand relaxed and balanced with the weight back.

2. *Contact:* Together shift the weight to the front leg, and forcefully thrust the hands on a direct line towards the pitch. Extend the arms. Hit the ball just in front of home plate.

3. *Turn Over:* After contact turn the top-hand wrist over the bottom (keep both hands on the bat).

4. *Release:* Extend the top-hand fingers outward and away from the bat (palm is down).

5. *Follow Through:* Swing the bat and arms up and around the head. While the bottom arm is leading the swing, the top arm should stay along for the ride.

Axe Bat

Age: 6 years and up.

Object: An Axe Bat can test for proper hand alignment in youngsters learning bat grip for the first time.

Equipment: An axe handle glued into the middle of a baseball bat sawed in half. The axe handle replaces the base of the bat.

Rules: Use wood glue and test the Axe Bat for strength before use. The batter swings the Axe Bat as if chopping a tree. For youngsters learning bat grip for the first time, stress the importance of lining up the middle knuckles (at least for hand position on contact), leading with the bottom hand, swinging down, and extending the arms.

Wrist Hitting

Age: 11 years and up.
Object: Yet another all-inclusive swinging exercise, the following is designed to develop strong wrists, a smooth swing, and bat speed.
Equipment: Bats for everyone.
Rules: Arrange the hitters in a circle or in lines. Use verbal commands for each drill. Work together. Include the following:

1. *One Hand:* Bend over with one arm behind the back, and a bat in the other hand (located in the center of the body). Smoothly flick the bat back-and-forth. The wrist should turn over fully. Keep the arm as straight as possible. Then switch hands.

2. *Two Hands:* Do the same routine as above except with two hands (i.e. as if chopping wheat with a sickle). The bat should go as high as the hips. Work on the wrist turn-over action.

3. *Figure 8:* Do the same routine as above but form a "Figure 8" with the swing.

4. *Circle Above Head:* Extend the arms out front, and circle the bat above the head (elbows away from the body). Keep the arms parallel and swing level.

5. *Shoulder-to-Shoulder:* Extend the arms out front, whip the bat from the back to the front shoulder. Swing hard and come back easy.

6. *Loop-and-Hammer:* Point the bat head at an imaginary pitcher. Take a normal swing. Whip the bat back and through in one big circular motion. It's almost two swings in one.
—Harvey Krupnick.

Big Bertha

Age: All.
Object: This exercise teaches proper bat size and grip. Bat speed, not

power, is the key for all good hitters. You don't want a bat too heavy or too light. It all depends on the strength of the individual.

Equipment: All kinds of bats: heavy and light, long and short.

Rules: First, hold a bat relaxed in the fingers. The grip tightens naturally on the swing. Second, test its weight by holding two different bats of choice out front with one in each hand. After a short time the heavier one should begin to dip. Then switch hands. Keep trying this until you can hold a bat in the dominant hand for at least one minute. Third, take an aggressive cut with this bat. Now try to check your swing before it crosses the front of home plate. If you can't, that bat is too heavy for you. Remember, swing the bat; don't let the bat swing you. Fourth, do 25 to 50 quality dry swings (no ball involved). See if the bat feels comfortable. Fifth, tell the kids to name their bat. The bat is your friend, so treat it that way.

Besuboru

Age: All.

Object: Certain ideals of Japanese baseball (Besuboru) center on relaxation and balance.

Equipment: Bats for everyone.

Rules: Hit as a group. Be "loosey-goosey" in the batter's box. Take deep breaths in and out. First, start by jumping up and down and then "stop." Everyone should be in an athletic and balanced stance. Second, take an aggressive swing and hold that position on the follow through for three seconds. Count out loud as a group. Third, put a hat on the floor. Put the shadow of your head inside the hat. Now swing. The head of the shadow should not come out of the hat (i.e. keeping the head down on the swing). Fourth, swing with your eyes closed. Fifth, swing in front of a mirror. Continually work on being relaxed and balanced throughout the hitting phase.

Big Mac

Age: All.

Object: This game is dedicated to Mark McGwire not only for his single-season home run record of 70, but also for his dedication to weight lifting. Stress the importance of an aggressive yet balanced swing.

Equipment: One bat per hitter.

Rules: Align the hitters in lines or in one huge circle. At a verbal command, swing in unison. Grunt while swinging. Then challenge the kids to swing harder and grunt louder. Do it again and again. Bats cost big bucks, so "get your money's worth." Then do the "swoosh" on another day. All at once take an aggressive cut. A soothing "swoosh" sound should be sweet music to the ears.

See, Read & Explode

Age: 9 years and up.

Object: As former major league hitting coach Mike Easler liked to say, batters need to "see" the pitch just before the pitcher releases the ball, "read" the spin and location of it while en route to the plate, and "explode" at a strike with an aggressive swing at the ball.

Equipment: Bats plus a brand-new regulation ball.

Rules: First explain "soft" and "hard" focus. While in the batter's box a hitter should first "soft" focus on the pitcher's head and shoulders. Then when the ball is just above the (baseball) pitcher's shoulder, he/she should "hard" focus on the ball just before delivery. Hammer home this theory in every live throwing activity.

Now arrange the group into lines. The instructor should face the team, and go through a simulated pitching movement. When the batter thinks the ball is just in front of home plate, he/she should take a swing. First, pitch in slow-motion for easy recognition. Second, pitch from the wind-up. Third, pitch from the stretch. Fourth, pitch full-speed. Fifth, add in the fastball and curveball (baseball only). See if the kids can pick up the different arm motions (fastball: thick wrist; curveball: thin wrist). Sixth, expose the kids to pitch location and react according (i.e. pull the inside pitch). End with a ninth inning, 3-and-2 count, 2-out, bases-loaded scenario.

—Mike Easler.

Soft Toss

Age: 6 years and up.

Object: When doing basic team hitting drills, set up stations where kids get a lot of swings while doing the different disciplines.

Equipment: Bats, balls and tee.

Rules: Pair the kids up and arrange five different batting areas with balls at each. During practice hit against the backstop or into nets. Before games, try hitting Wiffle (for baseball) or regulation balls (for softball) from the foul line directly into the outfield. Each of the following drills have a specific focus.

1. *Flips:* See the ball and hit the ball.

2. *Tee:* Think about hitting the ball in front of home plate. Later on add in middle, inside, and outside locations.

3. *Knees:* Kneel down and swing. Focus on rotating the hips.

4. *Step Hit:* Stride first and then swing. Keep the weight and hands back, and wait for the pitch (i.e. curveball).

5. *One-handed:* Hit down on the ball. Start with the arm in the launching position ("L") then explode down to the ball ("I"). Swing "L to I." Then switch hands.

Color Coded Hitting

Age: 12 years and up.

Object: Improve hand-eye coordination and quicken reaction time in order to consistently hit a variety of pitches.

Equipment: Bats, baseballs, pitching machine and L-screen (optional), white and yellow dimpled balls and white, yellow and red tennis balls.

Rules: As a warm up a pitcher flips a ball from each hand at the same time and instructs the batter to hit one of the two balls. For example, "High" for the high pitch, or "Low" for the low pitch. Another option is to use two different colored balls, with the batter instructed to hit one or the other. Advanced hitters can hit at balls numbered from 1 to 3 with the goal of calling out the number on the ball before contact. For the main drill, gather up three different colored tennis balls: white, yellow and red. Set up a close range batting practice session or short toss drill from behind a screen. The batter should practice a different hit according to the color of the ball. White means bunt (e.g. safe color). Yellow means curveball (e.g. caution), so the hitter should try and stay back and hit the ball the other way. Red means fastball (e.g. dead red) so sit back and rip! For further practice, perform a hitting drill with the pitching machine using white and yellow dimpled balls. Try hitting the white one and bunting the yellow. Or hit-and-run the white, and hit to the right side for the yellow. But stress the importance of picking the ball up as early as possible. These exercises work on improving hand-eye coordination through concentration (from release to contact), and the actual grip of the ball at the pitcher's "L" (focus upon release). Remember: Hitters shouldn't guess. These drills develop instinct and train the hands to react quickly and efficiently.

Donut

Age: 12 years and up.
Object: In honor of the Mariners' Edgar Martinez, this activity teaches bat speed in accordance with the "sweet spot."
Equipment: Bat, donut or Bratt's Bat, and balls.
Rules: Slide the donut onto the bat. Now take soft toss. The goal is to make solid contact on the "sweet spot." The donut serves as a guide while building up strength in the hands and wrists. It's also a great challenge. You can also try this with the Bratt's Bat (youth length/weight) and tennis balls. Instead of hitting with the donut younger hitters can tape over the "sweet spot" on a regular bat, so they know where to properly hit the ball.

Action Ball

Age: 6 years and up.
Object: Stress line drives, being aggressive on a two-strike count, and putting the ball in play. Never watch a called third strike. This indoor game encompasses quick at-bats with balls flying off of the floors, walls and ceilings.
Equipment: Bat and paper ball wrapped in athletic/duct tape.

Rules: The diamond can be set up (short distances between each base) if base runners are desired. The pitcher throws the paper ball slowly and over-hand from about 30 feet away. There are no home runs; only singles, dou-

PAPER →
&
DUCT TAPE
BALL

bles and triples. The instructor must keep track of "runner" location, number of outs, and score of the game. Ground rules are set up before play begins. Singles can only score a runner from third base. The hitter has a 2-and-2 count. Ball four results in a new count.

Outs include: (1) swings-and-misses, (2) foul balls, and (3) any ball fielded cleanly off of the wall, ceiling or floor. There are no force outs or tag outs. Batters hit and then must sit down in the makeshift dugout. Bench people must sit down against a wall in the assigned batting order. Everyone plays defense.

—Mike Andrews Baseball Camp.

Don't Miss

Age: 5 to 7 years old.

Object: This game is best suited for toddlers learning how to hit. It's also a great way to prevent them from throwing the bat.

Equipment: Tee, bats, balls, helmets, bases, cones, and bicycle tires or hula hoops.

Rules: Devise two teams. The batter hits off of the tee placed on home plate. If they miss the ball, or if they knock the tee over, this is a strike. Three strikes and you're out. They are also out if they fling the bat after contact. To prevent this, instruct the kids to place the bat in a bicycle tire or hula hoop just behind the plate. After a fair ball, he/she runs to first base.

You can also incorporate fielding and throwing exercises into this game. Place the tires or hoops (one for each fielder) adjacent to the defensive team (horizontal or zigzag). After retrieving the ball, players must run over and get into their tire or hoop. The ball must then be thrown and caught (overhand or underhand) in succession. While this is going on, the offensive team runs around a pair of cones. This scoring system stops once each fielder has caught the ball. The instructor should yell "stop" to halt the action.

Home Run Derby

Age: 10 years and up.
Object: This is a great game to test one's home run power.
Equipment: Balls, bats, tee, helmets, and home plate.
Rules: Scatter players around a fenced-in field. Batters receive three outs. A person could be three swings and out, or take 20 swings, for example. Any foul ball, swing and a miss, and grounders hit in the infield equal outs. Fair balls landing or caught in the outfield grass are singles (1 point). Balls reaching the fence on the ground are doubles (2 points). Balls hitting the fence in the air are triples (3 points). Balls going over the fence are home runs (4 points). Defensive players can catch fly balls for outs (optional).

For younger players, use second base as the home plate area. The object would be to hit balls over the fence. Pitch from the outfield grass or use the batting tee. If you don't have a fence, hit from the outfield towards the backstop. Count the number of balls you can hit high over the backstop. Try it as a competition.

Adults also play a slow-pitch softball version of "Home Run Derby." A batter keeps hitting until making three outs. Anything *but* a home run is an out. Only home runs count for points. Make the rounds more difficult by instituting the larger-than-regulation softballs.

Stadium Shot

Age: 8 to 12 years old.

Object: For the batter to hit the ball to the bleachers.

Equipment: Bats, home plate, and balls. Try this competitive hitting game on a football field which has stadium bleachers. Make sure the bleachers are vacant.

Rules: Hit towards the bleachers best served with a fence in front. You can hit off a tee, via soft toss, or short-toss BP. Each batter has ten swings. Points are awarded as follows: 1 point for a ball which rolls to the fence on the ground, 2 points for a ball which hits the fence in the air, 3 points for a ball which lands in the bleachers, and 4 points for a ball which goes over the bleachers. Kids love to hear the ball clang off the metal bleachers. After everyone has had a turn move kids closer to or further from the bleachers based on the score from their previous turn. The coach tallies individual scores. Shag once all of the balls have been hit. No one is allowed to field balls in the actual bleachers. Assign someone to collect the balls that go over the bleachers. You can use tennis balls, Incrediballs, or real baseballs.

Dinger Ball

Age: All.

Object: This game incorporates the value of hitting off of the tee.

Equipment: Tee, softball-sized Nerf ball, and four bases.

Rules: Make two teams. Set up four bases on a single basketball court. The batter hits the ball off of a tee and runs the bases. Upon retrieval the ball is then placed on the tee for the next batter, who swings away. Base runners do *not* have to advance, but may do so if they think it is safe. Runners cannot pass one another. There is no limit to the number of players on a base at one time. They may even make a chain to advance to the next base.

Players can be tagged out on pop-ups (caught off the wall/ceiling is an out too) or when tagged. There are no base tags, so it's non-stop action. If a player is declared out, he/she must cheer their team on for the rest of the inning but away from the action. This person may not bat again that inning. Players who make it home join the end of the lineup. Switch sides after three outs or when a team has no more batters—whatever the instructor decides beforehand.

If the batter hits the backboard with a batted ball, all bases clear and a home run is declared. The ball must pass half court and be in fair territory to be counted. The batter can only swing and miss twice or else an out is called. Once the ball is placed on the tee at home plate, runners may no longer advance and must wait until the ball is batted into play.

—Rules: Loren Sanislo.

Hitters Challenge

Age: 8 years and up.

Object: Hitters are challenged to see the ball and hit it hard. How hard they hit the ball, and where, dictates the points they receive.

Equipment: Bats, balls, helmets and gloves.

Rules: This game can be played either inside or outdoors while using a pitching machine or live arm. The hitter should aim to hit ground balls and/or line drives. Only fair balls count. Issue 7 to 10 swings each.

Hitter Scoring Includes:

    10 points: Line drive up the middle.

    5 points: Line drive anywhere else.

    3 points: Hard hit ground ball.

    2 points: Slowly hit ground ball.

    1 point: Pop-up/fly ball.

For another variation of this game, arrange a fielder at each position (no catcher) and rotate people after each hitter. Both hitters and fielders can now earn points on virtually every swing. Establish priority on subsequent grounders and fly balls. Try to maintain equal at-bats and fielding attempts at the different positions for each of the players. Include both of the scoring systems.

Fielder Scoring Includes:
>   10 points: Difficult catch of a line drive.
>   3 points: Difficult catch of a ground ball.
>   2 points: Routine catch of a ground ball.
>   1 point: Routine catch of a pop-up/fly ball.
> —Dave Smith and Bob Casaceli.

All World Hitting

Age: 7 years and up.
Object: Concentrate on making contact and hitting fair balls.
Equipment: Bats, balls, helmets and gloves.
Rules: This is a simple game for either inside or outdoors. It can be done with a pitching machine or through short toss. Use one hitter at a time with two on-deck hitters. Have everyone else situated around the field to collect the balls. A player simply keeps hitting until he/she fouls a ball off or swings and misses. Keep track of the number of fair balls they hit in a row. The "All World Hitter" is the one who has the highest number of consecutive fair balls.
> —Dave Smith and Bob Casaceli.

Hit the Fielder

Age: 9 years and up.
Object: This game aims at building confidence in relation to bat control and hitting to all fields. It also breeds strategy (i.e. with no outs hitting to the right side to move a runner to third base, sacrifice flies, or the hit-and-run).
Equipment: Various bats, regulation balls, tee, helmets and gloves.
Rules: Place at least one player at each of the seven positions (no catcher or pitcher). Hitters take their regular stance, and attempt to hit the ball off of the tee to a specific area. One must first call out where the ball is going to be hit. The ball can be hit in the air or on the ground. If a fielder has to move more than 5 to 10 steps back, in, left or right, then that fielder (closest to the area) gets to hit. If successful in hitting to that area, stay up. Be discreet in relation to these steps. You can only hit to each position once before a second round

can begin. After using the tee, try doing soft toss. Conclude with an instructor pitching to the batter.

Dome Ball

Age: 6 years and up.
Object: Even in limited space, play an indoor hitting game.
Equipment: Aluminum bat or broomstick handle, and Jugs foam ball or Nerf ball.
Rules: Make two teams; one hitting and the other on defense. Designate hitting

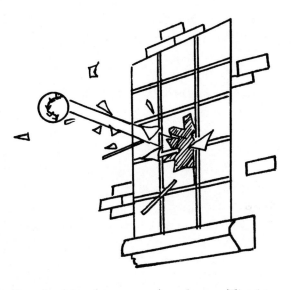

areas for safe hits (singles, doubles, home runs) and outs. The hitting team should sit on the bleachers or along the gymnasium wall far outside the field of play. Stress that these are simulated rules for games played in a domed stadium where fair balls could hit speakers, ricochet off of make-shift walls, roll into hidden crevices, or even get lost in the roof. Use a designated pitcher. Hitters receive one legal pitch. Name distinct foul lines and ground rules.

Outs include caught fly balls and swings and misses. Make no limits to foul balls. Home runs could be, for example, the walls at the end of the gym, doubles which reach the far wall, and singles which are not fielded cleanly. Make baserunning optional depending on space. Instructors are the umpires.

Rip

Age: 13 years and up.
Object: Create a fast-moving hit-and-run game in the gymnasium. Fielders better be awake for those "rips" right at them and the ricochets off of the walls.

Equipment: Tennis balls, bats, gloves, helmets, and pitching screen.

Rules: Provide a brief instruction of the hit-and-run play: swing at anything, use a shorter swing, and aim to hit ground balls to the opposite field. Have one batter at a time (standing in front of a wall) with a pitcher standing behind the screen near the middle of the gym. No catchers. Scatter all fielders behind the pitcher. Expect all types of pitches: fastballs, curveballs, change-ups, and pitches high, low, inside, outside, overhand and sidearm. Stress making contact at all times.

Start with seven swings apiece and then rotate. After a catch, roll balls off to the side, or to the vacated area in front of the pitcher. This keeps the game moving along and fielders focused on the hitter. Diving is encouraged. Have a second round when the batter stays up until he/she fails to execute the hit-and-run. Award bonus swings for hits to the opposite field. During the switch of batters (safety purposes) continually yell, "Watch the hitter!"

In Your Ear

Age: 7 years and up.

Object: Practice the proper technique for getting hit by a pitch. For youngsters and especially first-year players, kids need reinforcement of dealing with the fear of being plunked. Deal with this through a fun way of getting a "pitch in your ear." Try to instill this mentality: If grazed by a pitch in a game, act as if the ball never hit you, so you can continue to bat.

Equipment: Tape or Nerf balls, catcher's mask and helmet, batting helmets, makeshift batter's box, and bat.

Rules: On high inside pitches, instruct the kids to turn into the plate with their front shoulder. Keep the bat back and out of the way. Each person gets a turn. Batters have the choice of using a helmet or catcher's mask (depends on the age group, and strength/velocity of the throws). Align the kids in a circle around the batter, so balls stay within the group. The instructor should pitch. Throw balls at the batter both high and low. Follow this up with a "Dodgeball" activity where the batter is suppose to get out of the way of the pitch while staying in the batter's box. The batter can duck, jump, or "take one for the team."

Liner

Age: 8 years and up.

Object: Players can showcase their talents in a simulated "pressure" game. Swing at strikes, and hit the ball on a line. Fielders have less reaction time against line drives, especially at the "hot corner." Line drives also reach the outfield gaps quicker than ground balls or fly balls.

Equipment: Anything needed when a team is taking its swings.

Rules: Either have an individual or team competition: two random teams, starters versus non-starters, or position players versus pitchers. Fielders should spread out throughout the diamond. Hitters take 5 to 10 swings. No baserunning. The umpire verifies a successful line drive. Foul balls, swings and misses, and called strikes all count as swings. An instructor should throw (behind a protective screen) fastballs down the middle of the plate. Line drives, regardless of being caught or not, are worth a point. Avoid swinging for poor pitches.

Smelly Sock

Age: 9 years and up.

Object: On a rainy day play a fun game emphasizing bat speed, proper hitting fundamentals, hustle and sliding.

Equipment: Rolled up socks (game ball), bases and bats.

Rules: Best suited to wet grass; play either shoeless or in sneakers. Make two teams. The batter has a 3-and-2 count. Three outs per inning. Outs are recorded just as in a real game: force outs, catching a fly ball, strikeout, etc. There are no bases on balls. Home plate should be placed directly behind second base with the batter and pitcher both standing on the outfield grass. Align the other bases around the outfield.

The instructor is the umpire and should start as the pitcher. The sock should be pitched slowly and with a slight arc. Balls landing over the fence (if applicable) are home runs. Fielders (no gloves) should play their regular positions (switch each inning), and use game strategy. Sliding in the grass and diving for the sock are both highly encouraged.

This game is called "Smelly Sock" for three reasons. First, no one wants to hold onto a smelly sock for any period of time. Fielders should get rid of the ball quickly. Second, using the bare hands forces players to look the ball into their chests. Third, fly balls are frequently caught because a sock does not travel very far in the air. Just as in a real game, hitting down on the sock is the best bet for success.

Mano y Mano

Age: 9 years and up.

Object: "Mano y Mano," Spanish for "one on one," is a competitive game for the batting cage.

Equipment: Batting cage, pitching machine and balls, bats, helmets, and pitching screen.

Rules: This game is best played with 2 to 5 players per cage. Three outs per hitter (use balls and strikes). There are foul balls. One person hits at a time. Use the pitching machine. See how many runs you can score in a seven or nine inning simulated game. Bunting, sacrifice flies, and hit-and-runs must all be verbally called out just before the pitch is released. The on-deck batter serves as the umpire (i.e. determining singles versus extra base hits).

Pepper

Age: All.

Object: This traditional game works on bat control, hand-eye coordination, and fielding technique.

Equipment: Gloves, regulation ball, bat and plate.

Rules: A batter stands some 20 to 30 feet away from a group of fielders. One person tosses a strike to the batter who attempts to hit a ground ball. Batters should choke up and take a modified swing. Only hit strikes. After mastering the ground ball, add some competition. First, hit grounders to any particular fielder. Second, hit to players in a line going left to right or right to left. Third, call out the name of the person you're going to hit to. Fourth, fielders who make an error have to move to the end of the line.

After a swing-and-a-miss or line drive caught in the air, the person at the front of the line takes over for the hitter. The batter then goes to the end of the line and everyone shifts up a spot. A fielder can only go after balls hit to his/her area. All catches must be clean (no bobbles or traps). For that hitter who just seems to stay up forever, huddle up, and have everyone fake a toss with someone actually throwing the ball. It'll get the batter every time. Pitchers can play a hard-hitting game of "Pepper" to get accustomed to comebackers. For younger players, the instructor should begin hitting. Teams can also practice their bunting techniques in this game.

Rock Ball

Age: 7 years and up.
Object: This game emphasizes the hitting of line drives.
Equipment: Home plate, bat, small Nerf ball or Rag Ball, and cones.
Rules: There are two foul lines encompassing three "zones" (outfield, infield and pitcher). Defensive teams may place as many players as desired (up to 10) into either the infield or outfield zones. Defensive players may field balls only within their zones, and should switch zones each inning. Offensive teams may place any of its players as the pitcher (same team), and may alternate them after each completed at-bat. The pitcher must stay within the "pitcher's zone" the entire at-bat, and may deliver the pitch (over- or underhand) from anywhere inside that zone.

A pitch may be delivered as soon as all offensive players (except pitcher and hitter) are behind the "dugout line" (use equipment bags), regardless of the defensive team's readiness. A pitcher may stop any ball hit by the batter (same team) before it reaches the "infield zone" (ruled a foul ball). All offensive players hit in successive order regardless of playing infield, outfield, or sitting out. Reserves should take turns alternating into play each inning.

The home plate umpire calls outs, foul balls, zone infractions, home runs, and base hits. Offensive teams have three outs per inning. Each batter may receive up to two pitches an at-bat before being called out. Outs (adjust to skill level) include any swing and

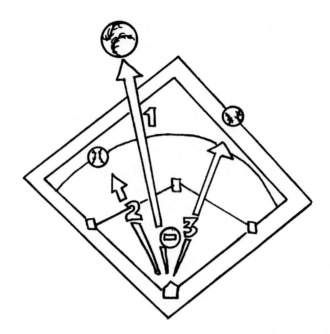

a miss, balls caught in the air, or any foul ball hit beyond the "pitcher's zone." Base hits include any fair ball dropping to the ground beyond the "pitcher's zone"; stopping within a fair "defensive zone" without being touched by the defense, or which is misplayed; or passing through the "infield zone." There are no doubles or triples. Home runs are any balls hit over an outfielder's head (umpire's discretion). No half-inning can last longer than five minutes or have more than five runs scored. No inning can start five minutes before the end of the "Rock Ball" time period (umpire's call). Both teams must receive equal offensive and defensive innings. All runs must be forced in.

—Mike Andrews Baseball Camp.

Splinter

Age: 9 years and up.

Object: In honor of the greatest hitter of all time, Ted "The Splendid Splinter" Williams, this game incorporates the different varieties of the base hit.

Equipment: Batting cage, pitching machine (optional), protective screen, balls, helmets, and tarpaulins labeled as "single," "double," "triple" and "home run."

Rules: See how many runs the batter can score in an inning. Three outs per person. Only line drives count as hits (singles: left or right of the screen; doubles: directly off of the screen; triples: back corners of the cage; and home runs: off the back of the cage). Tarpaulins (numbers for singles, doubles, triples and homers) can also be hung to designate the scoring areas. Each group has an equal number of hitters.

Anything hit off the top of the cage is an out. Depending on ability level, the umpire can give the hitter one pitch to look at prior to actual competition. Any pitch fouled off results in another pitch. Three fouls and you're out! Use tape hung on the cage to distinguish foul lines. Legal base hits must hit the sides, or end of the cage, in the air. However, a hard ground ball hit up the middle may be called a hit by the umpire. No double plays, sacrifice flies, or bunts of any kind. In order to "score" from second base, there must be a double, triple or home run. In order to "score" from first base, there must be a triple or home run. In order to "score" from third base, there must be a base hit of some kind. For week-long camps, keep league standings, and declare a "league champion" (each age group) or "batting champ." Multiple cages should each have an umpire who determines hits, runs and outs.

—A version of this game comes from the Mike Andrews Baseball Camp.

Target Practice

Age: 6 years and up.

Object: When without a partner, try hitting fundamentals with the backstop serving as "The Field of Dreams."

Equipment: Batting tee, bat and balls.

Rules: Face the backstop, and hit off of a tee while standing at home plate. Attempt to hit line drives off of the different squares of fencing: singles for the ground level squares (left and right field), doubles for the squares above the singles, and home runs to direct center field. Work on hitting to the different areas. Focus on "going with the pitch." Become that feared batter who can hit to all fields.

Name That Play

Age: 10 years and up (adjust to skill levels).
Object: If a hitter expects to execute in a game, one needs to practice those plays beforehand.
Equipment: Pitching machine, batting cage, bats, balls and helmets.
Rules: Simulate the many offensive strategies while batting against a pitching machine. Each discipline may call for a different batting grip, body alignment, position in the batter's box, and strength of swing. Use the following strategy. Progress in numerical order.

　　1. *Sacrifice Bunt:* Bunt a strike away from the pitcher.
　　2. *Drag Bunt:* Bunt a strike close to the foul line.
　　3. *Squeeze Bunt:* Bunt any pitch on the ground.
　　4. *Hit-and-Run:* Swing down at any pitch, and hit it on the ground.
　　5. *Move the Runner to Third Base:* Hit a strike to the right side.
　　6. *Sacrifice Fly:* Loft a ball to the outfield.
　　7. *Line Drive:* Rip a strike up the middle.

Try this game (older players) with a verbal command (particular play) just as the ball is shot out from between the pitching machine wheels. The batter must be quick and decisive just as in a regular game. If a batter is unsuccessful in executing a play, the next person hits. You can also perform "Name That Play" against a live pitcher. With hitting groups in the cage, have three stations: 1) live batting with the above scenario, 2) deciphering offensive signals from a coach (say what was called), and 3) standing in against a pitcher throwing on the side (no swinging).

Batting Practice

Age: 9 years and up.
Object: This activity is typically done at practice and during pre-game.

Vary the drills according to the age level. Designate a time frame (i.e. 30 minutes). Focus on hitting strikes up the middle and to the opposite field. And never swing and miss!

Equipment: Helmets, bats, fungoes, balls, bucket, gloves, portable backstop, and pitching screen.

Rules: Issue a number to each hitter or assign specific groups. Hit from the backstop or at home plate. Wear helmets. On-deck batters should chase foul balls. Have a specific format, for example:

1. *Sacrifice bunt.*
2. *Drag bunt.*
3. *Squeeze bunt.*
4. *Hit-and-run.*
5. *7 to 10 swings.*
6. *Run around the bases.*
7. *Lightning round.**

Hitting Tips: Work on individual weaknesses such as curveballs or outside pitches. To quicken a round of BP, bring the screen in closer to the hitter (called "Short Toss"). Try "Double-Barrel BP" with two pitchers behind two screens and two hitters. Alternate left- and right-handed batters on separate sides of the backstop. Throw to one hitter at a time. Older players can also hit with various BP rounds of seven, four, and three swings in each. "Early BP" is also popular in the major leagues. Lastly, let pop-ups drop before throwing the next pitch. Pitchers should throw the ball hard to simulate game conditions.

Fielding Tips: During BP hit ground balls to the infielders (focus first on the batter). Hit from the dirt cutouts in foul territory. Allow the pitcher to throw before hitting to a particular person. Hit pop-ups when switching groups. Everyone should play their desired defensive position. Have a "bucket person" collecting the balls behind second base.

---

*After the last hitter, bring all position players in to home plate. Batters get one strike, and stay up as long as he/she hits a line drive in fair territory. Outs include foul balls, called strikes, swings and misses, pop-ups, fly balls, and ground balls.

Shaggy

Age: 12 years and up.

Object: Pitchers aim to catch balls hit during batting practice and then throw the ball in a bucket. This activity gives the pitchers something productive and competitive to do during on-field BP.

Equipment: Infield and pitching screens, bucket, baseballs, and team hitting gear.

Rules: During on-field BP the large infield screen should be set up behind second base along with a bucket, and the pitchers scatter throughout the outfield. Players stay in their starting area, and aim to catch the balls hit in their direction. No interference allowed. Points are deduced for dropped catches. Points are awarded for catches and subsequent tosses toward the bucket. 1 point for a clean catch of a ground ball, 2 points for a clean catch of a fly ball or line drive, 3 points for a clean catch and then a toss which hits or rolls to the screen, 4 points for a clean catch and toss which hits or rolls to the bucket, and 5 points for a clean catch and toss which goes into the bucket. The person who has the most points when BP is done wins the game. *Note*: In pro baseball if a team throws a shutout the pitchers are awarded with on-field BP of their own.

Every Which Way

Age: 6 years and up.

Object: You want to get as many swings as possible in the shortest amount of time.

Equipment: Batting cage, tennis balls, two pitching screens, bats, blue tarpaulins, and mats or batting screens.

Rules: For an abundance of swings from close range, simply divide the batting cage in half. Use a batting screen or gym mat as the divider. Hang the blue tarps on the back sides of each end (better visual background). Set up two different pitching screens on each side. Have batters hit from the middle towards the backs of the cage, so balls are not hit in the same direction. Get 7 to 10 swings each, and then rotate to the other side. Instructors should pitch. Batters can work on different pitch types (fastball versus curveball), location (outside versus inside), or even against left- or right-handed pitchers.

Tee Ball

Age: 5 to 7 years old.
Object: Traditionally the game for first-year players.
Equipment: Tee, bats, balls, bases and gloves.
Rules: Make two teams. Name a batting lineup and fielding positions. Instead of pitching, the batter hits a ball placed on a tee at home plate. There are no strikeouts, so a batter stays up until contact is made. The batter should position him/herself just behind the tee. The catcher puts the ball on the tee for the next hitter. Put a fielder on the mound. Apply regular youth league game rules: three outs per inning, no leading or stealing, etc. Mention no throwing of the bat.

Sandlot

Age: 8 years and up.
Object: This is a game which tests one's hitting accuracy.
Equipment: Bat, ball, helmets, gloves, and four markers.
Rules: Set up the diamond in any setting. Use four cones or markers which divide the outfield into three zones: left, center, and right field. Make up a batting order, and arrange the outfielders between each zone. The pitcher should toss a pitch so the batter can hit it. The batter calls out the intended zone, and stays up as long as he/she can hit a fair ball to the designated area. You have to alternate the zones. One swing per pitch. The batter can let a poor pitch go by, but if you swing it counts as a try. No baserunning. Rotate the kids around between the outfield, pitcher and batter.

Billy Ball

Age: 11 years and up.
Object: Billy Martin, who took four different teams to the play-offs (Twins, Tigers, Yankees and A's), inspired his players to manufac-

ture runs. Use a similar offensive strategy of getting on base, advancing runners, stealing bases, scoring runs, and totally frustrating the opposition.

Equipment: Whatever used for a regular game.

Rules: Make up two teams. Then explain the many offensive strategies. For example: The walk and hit by pitch, sacrifice and drag bunts, squeeze and safety-squeeze bunts, fake and slash bunts, hit-and-run and bunt-and-run, delay, early and fake steals, sacrifice fly, hit to the right side to advance a runner to third, and the contact play with a runner at third base. An instructor should signal the plays to both hitting teams. The offensive team must attempt one of the above strategies for every base runner who reaches base (i.e. fake bunt and a steal). If successful three times in an inning (runner or runners must advance), that team is rewarded an extra out (three outs per inning). Tally up the successful plays and runs scored. The instructor can also reward extra outs for exceptional hustle and daring plays.

A team cannot run the same play twice in an inning. Repeated plays become outs. For those talented teams, offensive plays must then be made in consecutive order. Play this game depending on the situation, number of outs, and location of base runner(s). Walks, the hit by pitch, and defensive errors all count towards a successful play. The defense can use any means necessary to thwart the offense. Be daring but smart; aggressive not stupid. Push across the mentality of scoring runs even with two outs and no one on base. You'll achieve success by making every swing, every pitch, every catch, and every throw meaningful.

Trivia: Name the seven different ways to reach first base safely in a baseball game. *Answers:* 1) Base hit. 2) Fielder's Choice. 3) Hit by pitch. 4) Error by a fielder. 5) Dropped third strike by the catcher. 6) Base on balls. 7) Catcher's interference on the swing.

Combat

Age: 12 years and up.

Object: This drill is designed to improve bat control as the hitter practices a variety of offensive skills.

Equipment: Bats, real baseballs, and helmets.

Rules: At an outdoor practice a coach tosses BP from behind a screen. Assign two groups: batters and fielders, which will rotate after the first group of batters have had a turn. Infielders and outfielders set up at their positions, along with a catcher. Each batter attempts to hit four "missiles" attempting to consecutively do the following: 1) hit to the right side (to advance a runner to third base), 2) successful hit-and-run on the ground, 3) sacrifice fly deep enough to score a runner from third base, and 4) contact play (ground ball) to score a runner from third. Do not play the hits live. It works best if all the balls are picked up after every round. The focus of the batter should be putting the ball in play—good things usually happen when you put pressure on the defense. Each batter should keep a record of successful hits. This game can be played as an individual or group competition. A team may try a preliminary round, to help everyone get a feel for the game. You can also try a live game of Combat with runners and throws to bases. The goal of Combat is to survive and win!

Win It

Age: 10 years and up.

Object: Mold clutch players in practice.

Equipment: Bats, balls, helmets, gloves, bases, and pitching screen.

Rules: If a college softball game is tied in extra innings, a base runner is placed on second base to start the inning. Teams have a golden opportunity in which to score, and thus win the game. Here the instructor can design numerous situations in "Win It."

First, have a runner at second base with a hitter up at the plate. Arrange other players in the field. The hitter has one at-bat to drive the runner home. Play as if there were two outs. Second, use a bases-loaded situation where hitters and runners move up a base after a fair ball swing. This utilizes more players into the activity. Third, place a runner at third base with less than two outs. The batter must knock the run in either by base hit, sacrifice fly, ground ball (contact play), or squeeze bunt.

—Dave Wigren.

Steak Dinner

Age: 9 years and up.

Object: A batter's dream is to smash a line drive up the middle. A "steak dinner," the dream of all meals, is awarded to any hitter who can accomplish this act of great skill, marksmanship and accuracy.

Equipment: Tee, bats, balls, batting cage, and snow fencing.

Rules: Attach snow fencing across a batting cage about three-quarters of the way towards the end. Attempt to hit balls (tee or soft toss) off of the fence or to the back area. Points are awarded for line drives off of the fencing (1 point), the sides of the cage beyond the snow fencing (2 points), and the back portion of the cage (3 points). Grounders or balls hitting the top of the cage do not count. Five swings per hitter. Each group is divided into teams of 4 or 5 hitters each. Multiple cages should have an "umpire" or "judge" who tallies the results.

> —One part of this game comes from the Mike Andrews Baseball Camp.

Stickball

Age: All.

Object: This traditional game has been played in city streets, backyards, and in fields all across the country.

Equipment: Broomstick handle, and a racquetball, tennis ball, or spongy rubber ball.

Rules: The pitcher should bounce the ball in to home plate. One strike and you're out. Outs are only recorded on force plays and fly balls caught in the air. Play seven innings. Balls can be played off of walls or trees. If lack of space prevents the running of bases, simply play "Home Run Derby" rules. Remember, swinging a thinner bat at a smaller ball promotes hand-eye coordination.

Junk Ball

Age: 9 years and up.

Object: The Junk Ball Baseball has a dynamic "Air Baffle" design which acts like the seams on a real baseball ... only better! Just like the pitchers who cut or scuff baseballs, the air baffles do all the work. The Dial Your Pitch air ring controls the flow of air through the ball. Open holes allow more air to pass through the ball and that slows it down. The air baffles create resistance through the air and that makes the ball spin. The combination of these two forces and how the ball is thrown cause the Junk Ball to speed, curve, rise, drop, slide, and even float through the air.

Equipment: Official Junk Ball Baseball, 32-inch Sweet Spot Bat, bases, home plate, and pitching rubber.

Rules: Real baseball pitchers make use of the stitches or seams of a ball and a wide variety of throwing grips to put spin on the ball. If a baseball were smooth it would always travel in a straight line towards the batter. Baseballs have seams and these seams, plus a pitcher's throwing motion, cause the ball to spin against the wind as it travels through the air. There is a difference in the resistance of air around the ball, and the ball moves in the direction of least resistance toward the direction it is spinning. Speed has an effect on the ball's movement. The slower the ball is thrown the more spin can be put on it, and more spin equals more curve. The Junk Ball Baseball comes with scuff marks instead of seams and allows you to throw a fastball, curve, screwball (opposite curve), knuckler, rise pitch, sinker and slider. The scuff marks on one side of the ball disrupt the airflow around it. Air resistance is increased on the scuffed side and this causes the ball to move in the opposite direction. For the different pitches you can vary the following: grip, holes open or closed, holes held vertically or horizontally, with or without wrist snap, level of scuff marks (up, down, left or right), arm angle and speed.

To start the game mark off the dimensions of the playing field (best with an outfield fence). Determine single, double, triple, and home run lines. There is no running of the bases. All runners are imaginary. Runners advance when forced by walks or hits. A runner on base moves the same number of bases as the hitter (e.g. a runner on first advances to third on a double). Lines on the field indicate hits. A ball that travels on the ground past the singles line without being fielded is a single. A ball that travels in the air and lands past the double line is a double. A ball that hits the fence in the air without going over is a triple. A ball that goes over the fence on a fly is a home run.

Games consist of three, three inning games. Tie games go into extra innings. The team to win two games first wins the series. Games are 3 on 3, 4 on 4, or 5 on 5. Flip a coin to determine home team. There will be three outs per inning. Once a team is up by 10 runs or more, the game is over. A new pitcher must start each game and pitch at least one inning. Teams must announce the pitching rotation at the beginning of Game 1. Any combination of three strikes is an out. A strike is a foul ball, missed swing, or a pitch that hits the target (excluding the legs or base). Four balls are a walk. A pitch that hits a batter is a ball. If the ball misses the strike zone and the batter does not swing, a ball is to be called. Fast pitching is allowed. The pitcher must throw from the mound which is 46-feet from home plate. The pitcher must field the ball cleanly before it rolls past the mound for it to be an out. Ground balls must be fielded cleanly before passing the single line and before the ball stops moving to be an out. Bobbled ground balls are hits. A fielder is allowed one step in from the single line to field a ground ball. Ground balls that do not reach the single line are foul. Any ball caught in the air before it hits the ground (fair or foul) is an out. You may catch a ball off any object (e.g. tree or house) for an out. A ball hit into the trees or any structure and gets stuck, is an out. If bases are loaded and a runner on third is forced home, the defense may hit the target for the out. All players must bat. For further information and how to throw each pitch go to junkball.com.

Wiffle Ball

Age: All.

Object: "Wiffle ball" can be played anywhere. Recognizing the break of off-speed pitches (curveballs, sliders, knuckleballs, forkballs and change-ups) can be a great alliance to game conditions. Throwing a Wiffle ball is also the starting point for learning the grips, pressure points, arm speeds, and arm angles for the various pitches.

Equipment: Wiffle bat and ball, chair, home plate, two boundary markers, and bases (optional).

Rules: Try to make even teams. You must play bare-handed. Fielders can play anywhere but must be in fair territory. No "Indian Rubber" or baserunning. Name distinct ground rules, foul lines, a designated home run area, plus any automatic base hits. Use a five-ball, three-strike format. A chair serves as the strike zone, so no need for a catcher. A pitch hitting any part of the chair in the air is a strike.

Mark a pitching rubber (tape, chalk or stick), and have the pitcher throw from a close distance away. Place two markers behind, and to the left and right of the pitcher. Singles are any fair balls hit past the pitcher in the air which land before the markers. Doubles are any fair balls hit past the pitcher in the air which land beyond the markers. Home runs, for example, could be balls hit over some parked cars. Triples, for example, could be balls which hit the cars. Any ball hit in front of home plate which comes to a stop before the pitching rubber is a foul ball.

Balls caught in the air are outs. Fielders, including the pitcher, must field all ground balls cleanly to be an out. If not, an error is declared. Fielders can also turn a double play. After fielding a ball cleanly in a force situation, from that spot you can throw the ball at the chair. If it hits the chair, a DP is awarded. All runs must be forced in (i.e. bases-loaded single scores one). Similar to volleyball, rotate pitchers and positions each inning. For large groups, add in the running of the bases. Play a nine inning game, or try a week-long tournament.

Toddlers who have difficulty in making contact should use a batting tee (softball-size Wiffle ball) with the thicker Wiffle bat. Try lobbing a pitch to the youngsters (speeds the game along), and help the fielders get into positions (change each inning). High school and college players should switch hit when playing.

—Rules: Jack Janasiewicz, Bob DeMayo, Dave
Alexander, Chris Aufiero, and John Harley.

Hurry Up

Age: 8 years and up.
Object: This game preaches aggressive hitting and hustle.

Equipment: Stickball bat, four bases, and Jugs foam ball wrapped with athletic tape.

Rules: Make two teams and an assigned batting order. The pitcher is from the hitting team. This person cannot field any batted ball or else the batter is called out. The hitting team does not have to wait for the fielding team to get ready. Thus, the fielding team has to hustle out to their positions. The pitcher can stand anywhere, but has to be a safe distance away. The batter receives one pitch. A fair ball must be hit or else an out is called. No leading, stealing or bunting. It's great to see the kids hustle after each third out. They'll learn to place the next batter as catcher, so he/she can quickly jump into the batter's box. Runs are scored in traditional fashion.

Windex

Age: 9 years and up.

Object: Here the batter attempts to "spray" the ball to left, center, and right field. Remember, the hitter cannot control what the pitcher throws. React to the location of the pitch. By using the whole field, hitters can offset defensive positioning (i.e. pull hitter), and use the body more efficiently in "going with the pitch."

Equipment: Balls, bats, gloves, tee, helmets, and pitching machine (optional).

Rules: Arrange fielders throughout the diamond with one person batting. Hit using the tee, soft toss, pitching machine, or live batting practice. The ball should be located on the inside, middle, and outside portions of home plate. Attempt to hit strikes according to the location of the pitch.

Scoring includes:

3 points for a line drive.

2 points for a ground ball.

1 point for a fly ball.

When hitting against the pitching machine, crowd the plate for inside pitches, stand normal depth for middle of the plate pitches, and stand off of the plate for outside pitches. Someone should keep score. For individual work, place the tee on home plate and face the backstop. Hit to the left side, then middle, and end towards the right side. Then hit to the right, middle, and then left—hopping and moving with each discipline. Then mix the locations.

Right Field

Age: All.

Object: This game is designed to teach the line drive and how to play the various positions.

Equipment: Bases, gloves, balls, bats and helmets.

Rules: Have players take each of the positions 1 thru 9 (pitcher, catcher, etc.) on the diamond. If you have more than nine players simply use on-deck hitters and short fielders. Remember to give each position a number when dealing with toddlers. The goal is to hit line drives (no baserunning), and for the fielders to make clean plays.

Base hits and outs are recorded as in a real game. Hitters who get out then run to right field. A player who makes a throwing or fielding error also goes to right field with that particular hitter staying up. Everyone moves up a position in both cases; right field to center and so on. The lowest number always hits next. Players are running around the field, and each is learning a new position. The instructor can incorporate cutoffs if need be.

—Steve Coyle.

Run Home

Age: 8 years and up.

Object: Even a small group of kids can play a game which includes hitting, fielding, throwing and running.

Equipment: Bases, bat, ball, helmets and gloves.

Rules: Play with 4 to 10 people. You need a pitcher, batter, catcher, and at least one fielder. The batter receives a normal pitch from the pitcher. There are three varieties. First, with a small group (more open space) the batter must run around the bases before the ball can be returned to the catcher. Second, with a larger group the batter runs to first base and back to home plate. Third, narrow the playing field (i.e. triangle) by running to first base, to third, and then home.

Outs include: a fly ball (fair or foul) which is caught; swing and a miss; or a fair ball where the throw beats him/her back to the plate. Stay up until you get out. Set up a rotation system where players move up a position. With three fielders, the pitcher can cover home plate.

—Victor P. Dauer and Robert P. Pangrazi, *Dynamic Physical Education for Elementary School Children*, 6th ed. (Minneapolis: Burgess Publishing Company, 1979).

Crab Ball

Age: 9 years and up.
Object: For that rainy day, try an exhausting and challenging game in the gymnasium.
Equipment: Tee, bat, tennis ball, and bases.
Rules: Make three groups: outfield, infield and hitting. Rotate after three outs. Form defensive positions with as many outfielders as a team wants. Set up four bases (Little League-size diamond). Hit a tennis ball off of the tee. Game rules (including foul balls) apply except players have to crawl like a crab ("on all fours"), backwards or forwards, to the bases and while chasing the ball. Balls can be caught off of the walls for outs. No "Indian Rubber."

—Bill Mahoney.

Stand-Up

Age: 9 years and up.
Object: This game stresses a proper hip twist in the swing, and that aggressive first step in the field.

Equipment: Bases, bat, ball, helmets, gloves and towel.

Rules: Make two teams: one hitting and the other fielding. The hitter should bat from his/her knees. You can kneel on a towel. Fielders should also start kneeling down, and can only stand up once the ball is batted. Hitters should work on good hip rotation plus focus on putting the ball in play (i.e. ground balls versus fly balls). For the younger groups, the pitcher may be the only person allowed to start standing up.

Hey Batter, Batter

Age: 12 years and up.

Object: Both hitters and fielders need to be aggressive. And never take your eyes off of the ball—or balls.

Equipment: Two sponge or Nerf balls, bases, and stickball bat.

Rules: This indoor game adds a unique twist to a typical game. Make two teams: one hitting and the other fielding. But in this game use two pitchers and two batters. Pitch each ball at the same time. After contact the batter in the right-handed batter's box should run to third, to second, etc. The batter in the left-handed batter's box should run to first, to second, etc. Runs are scored after crossing home plate. Only fair ball hits should be played. Foul balls cannot be run out. Focus on making contact. Apply real game rules: force outs, tag plays, fly ball catches, etc. Fielders can make outs on any ball hit (exclude double plays). Six outs per inning. Try to have two umpires.

W.I.G.

Age: 6 years and up.

Object: "W.I.G." stands for "Wherever It Goes," stressing bat speed, aggressiveness, and speed on the bases.

Equipment: Handball (preferred) or Wiffle ball, bat, and two bases.

Rules: Pick two teams; one hitting and the other fielding (best suited for the gym). The batter has a 3-and-2 count. Three outs per inning. There are no walks—only strikeouts. The walls are in play. Bunting is allowed but no sliding or leading. Everything hit is a fair ball except for foul tips. The batter must attempt to hit a fair ball (not behind them). The instructor pitches. Home plate and second base are placed any distance away but in line with each other.

After contact hitters run to second base. Run to second and then home in one attempt, or stay at second and wait for the next batter to drive you in. Outs include: (1) ball caught in the air before hitting the ground, (2) batter tagged with the ball before reaching second base, (3) ball retrieved to second base before the batter gets there, or (4) force play when the ball is retrieved to home plate before the runner from second base gets there. A run is scored after one crosses home plate. A turn on the bases is over after reaching the plate. "W.I.G." may be a good way to get some sprints done. In this case simply increase the distance between bases.

Opposite

Age: 11 years and up.

Object: This game is designed to encourage kids to become switch hitters, and to use body parts they've probably never used before.

Equipment: Many varieties of gloves, bats, balls, helmets, and whatever used for batting practice.

Rules: Players must field with the opposite glove, throw with the opposite hand, and bat from the opposite side. Kids must also play positions they've never played before. The "best" skilled player has just as difficult a time playing as anyone else. The game only requires effort.

With shortages of a particular glove, instruct the players to field normally but throw with their non-dominant hand, a la Jim Abbott. For younger kids, play without gloves and use a handball. The pitcher can bounce the ball into home plate. Focus more on contact rather than power. For baserunning purposes, you can also make the kids run "in the opposite direction." To make the game even more intriguing, tell the kids to wear their clothes inside-out and backwards as well.

Backwards Baseball

Age: 13 years and up.
Object: Not a game for improving skill levels, but loads of fun especially for that off day during the week.
Equipment: Gloves of many varieties, bases, bats, helmets and baseballs.
Rules: Everything is done backwards. Start in the ninth inning. The ninth batter bats first. The first base you run to is third base, then to second, then to first, and then home. Thus, on a normal ground ball fielders need to throw to third base for a force out. You have to run backwards around the bases. Batters must switch hit opposite from their natural position. Fielders must field with their opposite glove and throw with their non-dominant hand. Shirts, pants, hats, and helmets must be worn backwards. It's four strikes for an out and three balls for a walk. Pitchers must toss with their non-dominant hand depending on the difficulty in throwing consistent strikes.
　　　　　　　　　　　　　—Bear Dunn.

Town Ball

Age: 6 years and up.
Object: "Town Ball" is one of the original names given to baseball in the 1880s. Here the kids take charge. Possibly on the last day of camp, tell the kids before lunch that they're going to be responsible for the rules (outs, batter count, ground rules, etc.) of the afternoon game.
Equipment: Game day equipment.

Rules: With kids coming from different backgrounds and neighborhoods, the group can learn new variations of pickup games. Let creativity run wild. As a youngster we had separate ground rules for my backyard: off of the house in center field (type of base hit depended on which section of the wall it touched); above, between, or off of the electrical wires (foul poles); the garden behind third base (never wanted to trample Mom's tomatoes); the huge apple tree in the third base line (if you ran into it, the tree always won); off of the neighbor's garden shed (we used it as first base, but you had to hurry up because the fellow usually took the ball from us); into the street (game off for oncoming traffic); and into the neighbor's uncut lawn in deep center ("The Corn Field" was an automatic home run unless you could find the ball in the long grass).

D.R.

Age: All.

Object: This game honors the spirit, devotion, and love of baseball played every day by youngsters in the Dominican Republic.

Equipment: Whatever type of bat and ball which you can make or find.

Rules: Play a game of ball anywhere. Carve a bat out of a tree limb or slab of wood. Use a duct-taped ball of newspaper or rolled up socks as the ball. Home plate may be a piece of cardboard. The backstop or strike zone might be a large retread tire. Bases could be trees. Forget about pricey equipment. Get out there and play!

Good Olde Days

Age: 10 years and up.

Object: This game brings us back to the turn of the century.

Equipment: Wooden bats, gloves, regulation balls, pine tar, bases, helmets, and possibly old uniforms.

Rules: If you can find the above equipment, try a game from memory lane. First, each kid must pick a player from the early 1900s. For those who have trouble remembering, help them out with names such as "Shoeless" Joe Jackson, "The Gray Eagle" Tris Speaker, "Gorgeous" George Sisler, Honus Wagner "The Flying Dutchman," Al "Bucketfoot" Simmons, Harry "The Slug" Heilmann, or "Wee" Willie Keeler.

The batting order should reflect the likes of, for example, Jimmy "The Iron Horse" Smith. More sophisticated kids can choose players according to their favorite position. Try to name their particular squad after a World Series champion from this era: The 1927 Yankees ("Murderers' Row"), 1918 Red Sox (last Boston winner), 1924 Senators (first and only title), or the 1934 Cardinals ("The Gas House Gang"). For some overnight homework, find some interesting facts and statistics about these earlier players and teams.

Second, apply old-time rules. For example, in the 1880s it was five balls for a walk and four strikes for an out. Wooden bats should be used. Show the kids how to apply pine tar. Wear the pants baggy and show a lot of stirrup. Break out the old gloves from the attic, and leave them in the field after each half inning. Batters should put their hat in their back pocket. No batting gloves allowed.

T-Ball

Age: 6 years and up.

Object: Not Tee-Ball in the original sense ("T" as in tennis ball), this game adds some spunk to the Wiffle bat.

Equipment: Wiffle bat, tennis ball, and duct tape.

Rules: Tape the "sweet spot" of a Wiffle bat with layers of duct tape. This makes the bat heavier and adds pop to the ball. Make the diamond any size you want. No gloves allowed. Fair balls must travel past the pitcher. Only one person can play at each infield position. You must have a catcher. The pitcher must lob the tennis ball to the batter. Make distinctive ground rules. Use a 1-and-1 count with an umpire calling balls and strikes. After ball four, the count returns to 1-and-1. A teammate would then run for you at first base. No "Indian Rubber." Traditional rules apply: tag outs, force outs, strikeouts, etc. *Note:* To "cork" the bat, pour sand into the top and then cover the hole with tape.

Whack

Age: 10 years and up.

Object: This is a fantastic drill to teach aggressiveness.

Equipment: Football tackling pad, bats, and duct tape.

Rules: Take an old football tackling pad or goal post protector, and wrap it with duct tape from top to bottom. Lean it up against the backstop or behind the dugout. It can even go with your team to away games. Have a hitter stand next to the pad, and take a full cut. Go one after another. Get the kids to really swing hard. You can write "hit me" on it for those who have no idea what the pad is used for.

—Mac Singleton.

Golden Chuck Bat

Age: 9 years and up.

Object: To throw the bat the farthest from home base. When frustrations are high try this activity to get a team out of a funk.

Equipment: Wooden bat, gold paint, and a magic marker.

Rules: In 1994 the Auburn (Mass.) Senior Babe Ruth team was having a tough season, and the kids weren't having a lot of fun. So I painted a wooden bat and inscribed "G.C.B." (Golden Chuck Bat) on it. Each hitter got up to home plate and threw the bat as far as possible. Who could toss it the farthest? Fling it to the heavens. Laugh the slump off by having a ball; sorry, throwing a bat. They did just that. I saw one my players from that team 10 years later, and he still remembered what this stunt did for the morale of the squad that summer. Here are a few other tips for recovery from a different season: use some gauze pads to "wipe the blood off the bats," or empty the bat bag to "wake them up."

Intrasquad

Age: 11 years and up.
Object: Here are some suggestions for a team scrimmage.
Equipment: Whatever used for a real game.
Rules: Divide the group in half or use teams of five players each. Then make set batting orders. Try starters versus substitutes, pitchers versus regulars, or the varsity versus junior varsity. Same rules as in a regular game. Use six outs per round. Batters must wear helmets. Each instructor should pitch for a different team. For older kids, mix in fastballs, curveballs, change-ups, and the ever dangerous lob pitch. Vary the pitch type and location. Umpires could be the catchers (each on a different team), or an instructor sitting in back of a screen behind home plate.

You can play a quick game with a 2-and-1 count. Two non-strikes equal a walk. Two strikes equal a strikeout. This prioritizes the need for first-pitch strikes from the pitcher, and for the batter to focus in on that first good strike. And for that last regular season practice, try a "Team World Series." Name two captains and have the kids pick the teams, pitching rotations, and starting lineups. Coaches also have to be picked (e.g. one person to oversee each team). Kids can come up with their own offensive and defensive signals, team T-shirts, and a friendly wager for the winning or losing team. Try to hire an umpire to do the game(s). Use a re-entry rule, official scorer, lineup cards, and attempt to play every kid on the roster. The team with the first pick is the away team. *Note*: College teams typically play a version of this for their last week of fall baseball (either best of five- or seven-game series).

Baseball Played With Re-Entry Rule

Age: 11 years and up.

Object: Re-entry and other alternative rules can increase the overall participation in baseball and softball.

Equipment: Equipment used in a traditional game.

Rules: Participation is of primary importance in youth sports, but baseball is the only game where kids cannot substitute for a player without being permanently removed for the remainder of a contest. The re-entry rule allows starters to withdraw from the game and re-enter once, providing such a player occupies the same batting position. A withdrawn substitute may not re-enter. A starter and his/her substitute cannot be in the game at the same time. A pitcher withdrawn from the game may re-enter in any position with the exception of pitcher as long as he or she was one of the nine starting players. A substitute may replace a substitute, and the starting player may still re-enter for the substitute. Re-entry allows more kids to play, games are more competitive, coaches can use more strategy, and the bench is more involved. After a while the rule becomes self-explanatory for the players and coaches. More importantly, they love it, especially at the summer all-star level where even good players are substitutes. It's good for the game to have these optional rules available. For additional strategies for increasing participation consider the speed-up rule (run for the catcher who reaches base), courtesy runner (can use one bench person per inning to run the bases), the DH (designated hitter) and the EH (extra hitter where the pitcher, and a tenth person all hit in the starting batting order). For quickening the pace of a game, experiment with these tactics: one foot in the batter's box on non-swings (if you swing you can step out), zero-pitch intentional walks, and possibly a time limit (clock on the outfield fence) for between innings (90 seconds) and between pitches (30 seconds).

Tournament

Age: Little League and up.

Object: To run an 8-team, double-elimination tournament.

Equipment: Equipment used in a traditional game.

Rules: The sponsoring host team typically gains automatic entry to the tournament. This team is responsible for an entry fee (e.g. American Legion State or Regional), staffing, concessions, and a grounds crew. The tournament committee handles all administrative duties (e.g. team rosters and birth certificates) and official scorekeeping. Have a staff orientation meeting, rain format (tarpaulins), purchase awards, and name an All-Tournament Team. Use a high-quality field with lights, good drainage and underground sprinklers, bullpens, warm-up area, covered dugouts, press box, electronic scoreboard, batting cage, ample bleacher seating, clean bathrooms, and plenty of parking. Devise a temporary website with game pairings and results, live updates, team stats, box scores, lodging, restaurants and directions. Some states arrange for house parents. Advertise in local newspapers and TV. Promote the tournament with signage throughout the community. Hire PA announcers and volunteer staff (parents and coaches) from the nearby youth leagues. Devise a spreadsheet schedule for volunteers to work (e.g. PA and scoreboard operators, grounds crew, foul balls, concessions, raffle, plus parking and ticket attendants). Hire quality umpires, a medical staff, and local police detail. Purchase plenty of regulation baseballs. Have a coaches conference call before Game 1 (plus a letter of welcome to entrants and contact information). Print up a game program with sponsor ads and scouting packets (rosters) for college coaches and pro scouts (for high school-level tournaments). Print up tickets, official T-shirts for staff, and badges for people working the event (e.g. press). Run a souvenir stand (sell commemorative T-shirts), silent auction of memorabilia items, and a 50/50 raffle. Put up open-air tents, and hang patriotic bunting. Field preparation should be done before all games (National Anthem) along with infield-outfield for both teams. Home teams should have a pre-determined dugout and wear designated uniforms. Post the times in the dugout for all pre-game activities (BP, IF-OF, field prep, ground rules and anthem). Organize an opening ceremony complete with a color guard and ceremonial first pitch. Some tournaments have a banquet and parade of teams.

A typical 8-team tournament runs Saturday to Wednesday. Four

games are played the first two days (9:30 A.M., 12:30 P.M., 4:30
P.M., and 7:30 P.M.). Losers of Games 1 and 3 play in Game 5
(Sunday 9:30 A.M.). Losers of Games 2 and 4 play in Game 6 (20-
to-30 min. after Game 5). Winners of Games 1 and 3 play in Game
7 (4:30 P.M.). Winners of Game 2 and 4 play in Game 8 (after
Game 7). In Game 9 on Monday (1 P.M.) the Game 6 winner plays
the loser of Game 7. In Game 10 (4:30 P.M.) the winner of Game
5 plays the loser of Game 8. In Game 11 (after Game 10) the winners of Games 7 and 8 play the final game of the day. On Tuesday
Game 12 pits the winner of Game 9 vs. the loser of Game 11 (4:30
P.M.). Afterwards Game 13 has the winners from Games 10 and 11.
Game 14 (4:30 P.M.) on Wednesday is the championship game (winners of Games 12 and 13). Game 15 (after Game 14) is only necessary if an undefeated team loses Game 14. Post and update this
bracket (banner) on the press box.

Showcase

Age: High school and up.
Object: The scouting of high school players is now big business. Major
    showcases include Top 96, Blue-Grey, Baseball Factory, Perfect
    Game, Blue Chip, SelectFest, College Select, Area Code Games,
    and Team One. It's an incredible opportunity to showcase one's
    skills in front of college coaches and professional scouts.
Equipment: Players bring their own equipment. The host should have
    a grounds crew, portable backstop, cages, infield screens, radar guns,
    cones, video camera, and stop watches. Use new baseballs, bring
    plenty of helmets and fungoes, and attract a company to supply new
    game bats. Side workout fields and a press box (PA) are a must,
    and have a field house in case of rain. Hire a trainer. Plan for a con-
    cession stand, bathrooms, and souvenir stand. Players should be
    issued a different colored T-shirt (numbers on front and back) and
    a showcase hat.
Rules: A showcase can be 1–2 or 3 days. Colleges (Divisions 1–2) use
    showcases as a tryout/recruiting camp. Some players are invited
    and most pay to attend. On the player biographical page include
    their team color/number, full name, position(s), home address/

phone number, height/weight, bat/throw, date of birth, graduation year, high school, and grades summary. Players are grouped into teams according to position to allow for equal participation (e.g. 20 per team). For no-shows and add-ons, include the information in the scouting packet just before the first session. Hire college coaches and staff to run the events. Payment should include work done with reimbursements for travel and lodging. Lunch can be pizza and drinks. Establish a website for registration and showcase events. A basic format (e.g. 8:30 A.M.-5 P.M.) includes baseline skills assessment, clinics, workout and evaluation sessions, specialized instruction sessions, and games. Start with a registration, player/parent orientation, and introduction of staff. The roster, duties, and schedule should be printed on a spreadsheet. Coaches should wear their school gear. Players work out according to their team color and in numerical order (so evaluators can follow the rosters easier). After stretching players are timed in the 60-yard dash. Sprint from the steal position with a go-signal.

After a throwing warm-up players go through a defensive workout (actual fungoes) to test for arm strength, accuracy, and pop time (catchers). Outfielders throw from right field to third base and then to home plate (two to each base). Infielders throw five times from shortstop to first base (two from regular depth, one left and one right, and a slow roller). First basemen throw to third base. Catchers (in full equipment) get five throws to second base (times recorded) plus assessment on framing, blocking, and fielding bunts. For on-field batting practice (close range) hitters receive 10 swings each, and run to first (timed) after their last swing. One team should hit as a group with another shagging in the outfield (elite programs use wood bats). During hitting, separate clinic sessions can be occurring at other sites around the outside of the field. These rotating sessions (30 to 45 min. each) can include base running, bunting, infield and outfield play, catching, strength and conditioning, hitting and cage time, pitching and PFPs (try for equal numbered groups). Thus, players are learning from coaches—not just trying out. Keep in mind that players are being evaluated at all times which means hustle, look good in the uniform, learn and improve and play hard. Moreover, the format should allow for individual assessment by the evaluators at any one time (e.g. announce the player hitting BP). Specialized video (additional charge) can be taken of the defensive, hitting, and pitching stations (sent later in the mail). An instructor can sit alongside and analyze the mechanics in slow-motion (optional voice-over) and compare with a split-screen of a MLB player. Radar readings (arm speed and velocity) are done on infielders, outfielders, catchers and pitchers (bat speed can be tested via contact in live BP or off a tee). The pitchers work out initially in the bullpen: fastball, slider/curve, and change-up both from the wind-up and stretch. Let the catcher know which pitch is coming.

Individual evaluations (equally distributed amongst the staff) should be done with each participant (with a written results/comments page for each section). Pitchers are evaluated (with radar readings) on their bullpen session (balance, hand separation, stride/direction, arm action and slot, extension, and follow through), and game performance (movement and command for each pitch, and mount presence). Ratings are noted 1 thru 5 (5=exceptional, 4=above average for high school, 3=average, 2=below average, and 1=needs improvement). Similar ratings occur for position players: fielding (foot work, fielding skills, exchange/release, arm strength, accuracy, and arm speed), catchers (practice and game pop times, footwork, exchange/release, arm strength, accuracy, receiving, blocking, and arm speed), hitting (balance, bat speed, power, and swing path), and running (60-yard dash).

The nine-inning games (with umpires) last 2:45 each with field prep in-between. Players warm-up on the side before competition (45 minutes prior), and should be ready to go when the previous game ends. The home team for the next game takes the field immediately after the completion of field prep. Sprint on and off the field. Showcase staff can coach the games, or evaluate at home plate behind screens. Here are some general rules: There is always one out (even after an out is recorded). Five-to-seven hitters bat every inning (always green light) as determined by the play list posted in the dugout. Make all plays on the last batter of the inning. Players play defensively at the position and in the inning listed on the play list. Primary position players get 3 to 4 at-bats (min. three defensive innings), and primary pitchers get 1-to-2 innings of work (five warm-up pitches). Secondary position players (pitchers first) get 2-to-3 at-bats, and secondary pitchers (regulars first) throw one inning. All hitters start with a 1-and-1 count. Hitters must step into the box when the catcher throws the ball to second base (to start the inning). If a batter walks or gets hit by a pitch, the count is re-set to 1-and-1, and a runner is placed on first base (from coaching box). Hitters take first base on a third walk or hit by pitch. A base runner must steal second base on the first or second pitch (if second base is unoccupied). In this situation the pitcher must use the slide-step, can only throw over once, and may not pitch out. During attempted steals, catcher pop times are being recorded. No more stealing after the catcher has had two pop times recorded. If the first three batters of the inning do not reach base, then a runner is placed on first. Catchers can throw down to second base, but the ball must be returned directly to the pitcher; after defensive outs as well to keep the game moving. Umpires typically work two straight games (home plate and bases). Awards can be given out to Most Outstanding Player (Hitter, Pitcher, Defense), and to best 60-time and radar readings. Lastly, the showcase should include the following information on their website: application/registration instructions, rosters, clinic format/dates, location/directions, colleges/scouts attending (mention throughout the proceedings), daily schedule, FAQs, hotel/travel, lead instructors, NCAA compliance, photo galleries, participation waiver, position availability, refund policy, testimonials, video analysis, and weather policy.

Twelfth Man

Age: 8 years and up.

Object: You can play situational games even with a small group of people.

Equipment: Anything used for a regular game.

Rules: Most Little League teams have 12 people, at the most, on a single squad. Intrasquad games are quite difficult and sometimes impossible to play. Thus, make three teams with about four people in each. Team 1 hits and runs the bases. Team 2 plays the infield which includes a catcher. Team 3 plays the outfield which includes the pitcher. You must bat in the assigned order. If a turn at-bat comes when you're on the bases, a teammate not on the bases must take your spot. The teams rotate after three outs. Move from the outfield to the infield, infield to hitting, and hitting to outfield. An inning is over after each team has batted. Everyone must pitch. Pitchers are limited to one inning at a time.

Gas Master

Age: 12 years and up.
Object: Challenge the kids to hit against the hardest thrower around.
Equipment: Helmets, bat, Rag Ball or Incrediball, and catcher's equipment.
Rules: An adult, instructor or college pitcher should throw from the

mound. Make an announcement on the PA system as the "Gas Master" walks from the bullpen or out of the woods. The pitcher throws as hard as possible: fastballs, breaking balls, etc. Each batter must attempt to make contact against the "Gas Master." Have the kids go one at a time. Tell the youngsters not to be afraid of the blazing pitches. For safety reasons use a soft-surface ball. Older players can try this activity against the pitching machine (on maximum velocity). For a backyard game, try hitting a tennis ball with a wooden bat. See how hard you can throw it, and how far you can hit it.

—Dave Smith, Bob Casaceli, and Jack Janasiewicz.

Body Double

Age: All.

Object: Try to imitate the stances, swings, and mannerisms of famous major leaguers.

Equipment: Bats.

Rules: When I was a kid, we all tried to copy the swings of Carl Yastrzemski, Reggie Jackson, and Rod Carew. Do the same today. My favorites are Ken Griffey Jr., Nomar Garciaparra, and Mark McGwire. Take turns by trying to guess the big league hitter. Whoever correctly names the person then gets to become the "Body Double." You can also mimic a person's walk, fielding ability, or pitching mechanics. *Note:* Youngsters should never try to be someone else during a game. Develop your own skills and talents which work for you!

W.A.N.D.Y.

Age: 9 years and up.

Object: Similar to the basketball game of "H.O.R.S.E.," this is a test of one's batting accuracy.

Equipment: Bucket of regulation balls, bases, and bats (preferably fungoes).

Rules: Hit from home plate. Play with two people or a group. The object is to hit balls to a designated spot on the diamond. Call out the play before swinging. If the initial hit is successful, the next person must repeat the play. If that subsequent hit is unsuccessful, a letter is given to this person. Once "W.A.N.D.Y." is spelled out, that person is eliminated. Obviously the initiator of the game rotates after unsuccessful attempts.

Try pop-ups aimed at the different infield positions. Who can land a pop-up in the batter's box? Hit a grounder or line drive off of a bag. Drive a ball over the fence or possibly off of a billboard. Lace a one-hopper off of the infield dirt which caroms into the outfield grass. Switch hit, or whack two balls at once. Be creative and see who is the best at "wielding the wand." Remember that a swing and a miss counts as a turn as does anything which does not meet the called play. This is a great game for coaches who have some time to burn before practice.

Baseball/Softball Golf

Age: 10 years and up.

Object: This game works on bat control, hand-eye coordination, and hitting the ball to all fields.

Equipment: Bats, balls, various pieces of equipment, pen, paper and tape.

Rules: Apply the rules of golf to a baseball or softball diamond. Designate areas around the field as "holes," such as a fence post, dugout wall, base, helmet, glove, or an actual drinking cup. Use a piece of paper with a number on it to decipher the different "holes." The object is to hit the ball to the "holes" in the fewest amount of attempts possible—either out of your hand or while the ball is on the ground. Wherever the ball stops after each shot is where the player has to hit from. You can putt the ball on the ground when need be. A hole is completed when the ball actually hits or goes into the target. Have as many "holes" as you want. Keep a personal scorecard.

Tennis Baseball

Age: 8 years and up.

Object: This hitting game is designed for a small group of players with an emphasis on making contact with the ball.

Equipment: Tennis racket, tennis balls, and bases. A baseball field with a pitching rubber on the mound.

Rules: Play 5 on 5 at a Little League field. Use tennis balls instead of baseballs, and a tennis racket instead of a bat. Gloves are optional. Play a traditional six innings with three outs per team. Outs include caught fly balls, force and tag plays, and strikeouts. Foul balls with

two strikes also count as strikeouts. No walks, and no bunting. The goal of the pitcher is for the hitter to make contact with the ball. Thus, don't fire the ball but also don't lob it—somewhere in between. For 3 on 3 use "pitcher's poison" where force outs can also include getting the ball to the pitcher who is standing on the rubber with the ball before the hitter reaches first base. For a game with an odd number of players use an "all-time pitcher" (same for both teams), or require the batter to hit to the opposite field. Younger players can also try hitting the ball out of their hand from home plate. You can vary the rules and hitting count every time you play.
—Rusty Eggen.

Olympiad

Age: 9 years and up.

Object: This could be the concluding event of a week-long camp or class discipline. Depending on time, space, and available equipment incorporate as many skills as possible into an Olympic-style competition.

Equipment: Balls, bats, gloves, helmets, bases, stop watch, and Radar Ball and Canvas Catcher (if applicable).

Rules: Have an instructor in charge of a specific station who records the times/results for each participant. Do not reveal any scores to the kids. Players rotate from station to station while competing against themselves or against other teams of similar age. Players earn points for successful plays in the Hitting, Bunting, Jumping, Pitching 1, Infield, and Outfield stations. The Top 5 finishers pertain to the Running, Throwing, and Pitching 2 stations.

Points, either 5, 4, 3, 2 or 1, would only be added to the scores of the top 5 in those three stations. Even if someone has a poor showing in one area, they always have a chance to do better at another one. Tally up the scores at lunchtime. Announce the champions (each age group) at the end of the day. The camp can run an "opening" and "closing" ceremonies, allow the kids to pick a country name for their team, and award medals (i.e. baseball cards or ribbons) for the winners.

The skills format of "Olympiad" includes:

Running: Fastest times home to first and first to third.
Hitting: Line drives in a 5-pitch batting practice.
Bunting: Bunts within markers in a 5-pitch scenario.
Jumping: Catches of 3 balls thrown high over a fence.
Throwing: Distance throws (3) measured on a football field.
Pitching 1: Throws (5) into the Canvas Catcher net.
Pitching 2: Velocity (5 throws) on the Radar Ball.*
Infield: Clean catches of 5 ground balls.
Outfield: Clean catches of 5 fly balls.

*The Radar Ball clocks speeds up to 105 mph either from 46 feet (Little League or softball) or 60 feet 6 inches away (high school baseball and up). As a substitute one can purchase a radar gun.

Survivor

Age: 9 years and up.
Object: Spice up a camp week with a series of physical and mental challenges based on the hit reality TV show.
Equipment: All kinds of baseball equipment (equal items per team), buckets, helmets, catcher's gear, bases or cones, bean bags or softie balls, colored construction paper, corkboard or plywood, saw, and fungoes or wooden bats.
Rules: Divide the kids into equal teams. Use team names, slap on some eye black (e.g. tribal war paint), and dress up in distinctive uniforms. One counselor or coach should join each team. Each player must compete in every challenge. Depending on space and time you can have 5–10 challenges. Create a tiki idol-like statue, and award it to the winning team after each competition. Here are some challenges along with simple rules. *Fireman's Bucket Brigade*: Use an equal number of balls per team. Have a starting and finish line for each team. One person starts the balls. If you drop the ball you can't use your hands to pick it up. The chain stops until a dropped ball is put back into play. The game is over once all the balls reach a bucket at the end of the line and everyone is sitting down. *Tower*: Build a tower with a bunch of baseball equipment. Set a time limit with a countdown to the last minute. The highest standing tower wins. *Word Scramble*: Spell out a word(s) related to baseball (e.g.

All Star Game or George Herman Ruth). Provide a hint to start. Letters go on colored paper with a different color for each team. Start by hiding letters in the woods or athletic facility (e.g. treasure hunt). Set a time limit. The first team to spell out the word(s) wins. *Ball Toss*: Use bean bags or softie balls. The target can be made of corkboard or plywood. Hang the target on a fence. Cut a small circle at the top for the balls to go through. Put a barrier (cones) down for people to throw behind. Three chances for each person in line. Throw it like a ball or toss it like a dart (accuracy over velocity). The first team to 21 wins. *Relay Race*: Run with a ball balanced in the hollow end of a wooden fungoe or bat. Go down and around a cone and back to your team. You can only run if the ball stays in the hole.

—Karyn Wigren.

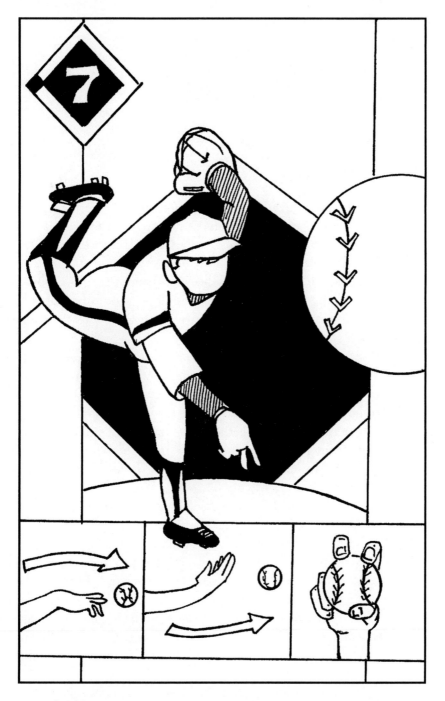

Throwing and Pitching

Boys would be big leaguers. As everybody knows, but so would big leaguers be boys.—*Philip Roth, author of* The Greatest American Novel

THE BASICS

Throwing: Get a firm but relaxed four-seam grip (letter "C") on the ball. Put the first two fingers a half-inch apart on the seams with the thumb directly underneath. Turn the left shoulder towards the target (for right-handed throwers), and bring the glove and ball up to the right shoulder. Separate the ball from the glove somewhere between this transition. Take a shuffle-step or crow-hop, and rotate the hips around (chest is facing target). Step directly to the target.

Think of bringing the ball down, back, and above the ear. As the arm starts forward keep the elbow up and glove parallel to the ground and tucked near the chest. Push off from the back side. Throw with an overhand whipping motion, and release the ball in front of the body and directly at the target. Snap the wrist down (i.e. pulling down a shade). Thrust the glove-side elbow away from the body. Allow the back foot to come around. Let the body follow in the direction of the target after release.

Specifically, infielders need to get rid of the ball quickly. Outfielders can afford to crow-hop and make a bigger arm circle. In a game always throw the ball hard, and try not to aim it.

Pitching Overhand: Use the overhand delivery for purposes of velocity and control. Grip the ball with the fingertips. Take a signal from the catcher. The pitching motion starts with the wind-up (no one on base). While standing on the rubber (right side for right-handers), take a small step backwards (glove-side leg). Pivot the throwing-side foot parallel to the rubber. Now lift the stride leg upward at hip level (higher for older players), and break the ball from the glove.

At the start of the stride, bring the ball down and back (start of the arm motion). Thrust the stride leg directly towards home plate. Initially keep the front foot closed then open it when the hips begin to turn. During the stride bring the ball back and then forward in one continuous motion (fingers on top of the ball). Land flat-footed (knee bends), and in the same area with each pitch. When the front foot hits the ground, the back arm should be shaped like the letter "L" with the ball located above the throwing shoulder. The glove-side elbow is thrust away from the body, and the hips turn.

As the weight shifts from the back to the front, the arm is coming forward and snaps across the body (complete circle). The ball is snapped downward and released in front of the face. Arm speed may depend on the type of pitch. Upon follow through the back leg is released from the rubber. This squares the pitcher to home plate for a proper fielding position. Focus on the target during the entire phase. Use a plate when throwing to a catcher.

Pitching Underhand: In *slow-pitch*, the arc of the pitch should be at least six feet and not more than 12 feet from the ground. In *fast-pitch*, the ball travels virtually in a straight line. The *slingshot* style is a slow backward armswing with a fast, forward swing and release of the ball. The *windmill* style is a complete arm circle.

Start with the ball (proper grip) held in front of the body for at least one second. Take a signal from the catcher. Stand with the push-off foot in front of and touching the rubber, and the striding foot in back of or on top of the rubber.

For the *slingshot*, the arm swings directly backward (slightly bent with wrist cocked) with the body rocking back on the legs. For the *windmill*, the arm swings forward and upward (slightly bent with wrist cocked). Instead of rocking back, the front leg is lifted up to stride forward, and the weight shifts to the push-off leg. During the downswing for the *slingshot*, the body pushes forward, the front leg strides to home plate, and the arm swings in a downward arc. During the downswing for the *windmill*, the glove-side foot strides to home plate, the body pushes forward, and the arm swings back and down in a complete circle. Upon release for both varieties, snap the wrist forward and release the ball from the fingers while the back foot leaves the rubber. In the follow through, the pitching arm continues upward until the elbow bends and points at the catcher. The push-off leg steps through in front of the striding leg. Use a plate when throwing to a catcher.

TEAM THROWING DRILLS

Age: All (perform long toss after age 10).

Object: During a throwing session, accomplish the many variations. First work on proper techniques, then loosen the arm up, progress to long toss, and conclude with throwing by position and specialties.

Equipment: Balls and gloves.

Rules: Partner up. One group should stand on the foul line with plenty of space between throwers. Continue at each formation until the leader switches the discipline. Include the following:

    1. *Wrist Flicks:* Grip and then flick the ball (wrist snap).

    2. *High T:* Pivot the body and form the letter "T" (i.e. arms away from the body) before throwing.

    3. *Bury Front Shoulder:* Swing the glove away from the body and then throw (emphasize a complete and downward follow through).

    4. *Catch:* Receive the ball with two hands and then throw.

    5. *Throw:* Throw back and forth in one continuous motion at about half-speed. Take one step towards the target. Never start off flat-footed. Softball players can alternate between overhand and underhand throws.

    6. *Long Toss:* Slowly increase the distance between throwers. Look to get "air" under the throw. Receivers act as the cutoff person.

    7. *By Position:* Outfielders use the crow-hop before throws. Infielders and catchers play quick toss.

    8. *Specialties:* Outfielders do self pop-ups before the throw. Infielders do tag plays. Catchers work on framing, and then throw from the crouch.

TEAM PITCHING DRILLS (OVERHAND)

Age: 9 years and up.

Object: During a pitching session, accomplish the many variations. First work on the proper techniques, then loosen the arm up, progress to long toss, and conclude with specialties.

Equipment: Balls, gloves, and home plates (can also use white towels).

Rules: Partner up. Start with the proper grip while holding the glove out front just under eye level. Continue at each formation until the group leader switches the discipline.

Points to Consider: Turn with the ball and glove, make a smooth transfer behind the back, get the ball above the throwing shoulder, rotate back, tuck the glove, snap the ball out from beyond the head, continue the body forward, swing the back leg through, and be in a balanced fielding position. Perform each drill according to the desired discipline, each completed with a throw.

1. *2 Knees:* Work on the hip pivot.

2. *1 Knee:* Glove-side foot in front; work on bringing the ball back and up.

3. *1 Leg:* Glove-side leg in front with a wide stance; work on transfer and swinging the back leg through.

4. *Stretch:* Feet shoulders' width apart facing either first or third base; work on striding to the plate and weight shift.

5. *Wind-up:* Work on a small step back, the balance point, and coordination throughout.

TEAM PITCHING DRILLS (UNDERHAND)

Age: 9 years and up.

Object: During a pitching session, accomplish the many variations. First work on the proper techniques. Loosen the arm up by throwing the ball overhand, and conclude with the underhand specialties.

Equipment: Balls, gloves, and home plates (can also use white towels).

Rules: Partner up. Start with the proper grip. Continue at each formation until the group leader switches the drills.

1. *Wrist Snap Drill:* Have the pitcher and catcher come together about 10 feet apart. Practice cocking the wrist back, and snapping the ball forward. Leave the side of the wrist against the thigh.

2. *Slingshot Drill:* Bring the arm above the head with a slightly bent elbow. Throw the ball with a snap at the hip, and practice the follow through. The follow through finishes with a bent elbow facing the catcher.

3. *Thrust Drill:* Practice pushing/thrusting off of the back drive leg towards the catcher.

4. *Slingshot Pitch:* Warm up while using the full leg and arm motions in a slingshot style.

5. *Windmill Drill:* Rotate the arm in a full windmill circle while the feet remain still. Practice with the arm following through.

6. *Windmill Pitch:* You are now warmed up properly. Begin windmill pitching.

—Rachel Economos.

THROWING AND PITCHING GAMES AND ACTIVITIES

Grip It

Age: 9 years and up.

Object: Learn the basic pitch-ing grips without tele-graphing the pitch to the batter.

Equipment: Balls and gloves.

Rules: Arrange the pitchers in a line. At the signal, have each person grip the ball according to the call (*base-ball:* four- and two-seam

fastballs, change-up, curveball and slider; *softball:* fastball, curve-ball, change-up, in-shoot, drop and rise). With the glove in front of the face, grip the ball without moving the mitt. The instructor should watch each phase of this activity from behind the group. Then have each pitcher perform this drill with a live toss to a catcher. *Note:* Little League pitchers, for example, should try and master 2 to 3 pitches.

Movement

Age: 11 years and up.

Object: Pitchers strive to add movement to their pitches and variety to their pitching repertoire.

Equipment: Game balls and gloves.

Rules: Pitchers should play catch with another pitcher as part of the daily warm-up. Pitchers throw from the mound with the goal of adding late movement to each pitch—either in and out or down (away from the batter's hands). To add movement to the pitch use different grips (fingers on or off the seams), vary ball placement in the hand (e.g. choke it for a changeup), and use different pressure points on the ball, applying more pressure for increased movement and less for more velocity. Changing speeds with breaking pitches (changeup, curve or slider) can throw off a hitter's timing, especially his/her stride. Pitchers can focus on developing their aptitude for the essential skills of pitch selection and focus, control (strikes) and command (location), movement and changing speeds, velocity, and getting people out. These skills can be developed in a variety of ways. Experiment each day with a different grip, ball placement, or pressure point. Keep the same arm speed but use a different arm angle. Try for movement with a different pitch on each throw. Ask hitters for feedback. See what the other pitchers on your team are doing. Work with the coaches. Always maintain proper mechanics, balance, and follow through when performing any type of pitching drill. And remember that the most important pitch is Strike 1!

Elimination

Age: 10 years and up.

Object: Use this as a competitive game during long toss. Stress accuracy and proper throwing technique, especially the follow through.

Equipment: Gloves and balls.

Rules: One partner stands on the foul line and the other in the outfield. The instructor initiates each toss, and designates the location of the outfield group. You can only take three steps before throwing. Receivers must catch the ball without it getting by them. You can scoop the ball. Older groups can only take 1 to 2 steps to make the catch, and must not drop the ball. Keep moving back equal steps when groups successfully throw and catch the ball. Use listening skills such as ousting those groups not throwing on the whistle or call. Eliminated groups (sit down) should act as assisting judges. Change partners each day.

You can also vary the rules by allowing up to three steps for the catch. Then try a long distance throwing contest only. Rotate the throwers and then receivers. See which person can throw the ball the farthest. Also, if a ball gets by a receiver that person must throw from the spot where the ball is retrieved. For safety reasons make sure eliminated people watch the action away from the field.

Bull's-Eye

Age: 9 years and up.
Object: Work on pitching accuracy either overhand (baseball) or underhand (softball).
Equipment: Balls, hanging target or tire, and chalk.
Rules: Hang a bull's-eye target (circular or square) on a wall or soft toss net. Use numbered areas to designate a point system. Stress proper mechanics. Youngsters everywhere have also thrown balls at a hanging tire. For a pickup baseball game in the schoolyard, simply draw a strike zone on a wall in chalk. Make the lower portion about 18 inches above the ground, 19 inches wide, and then 42 inches high. A batter is called out for any ball which hits inside the "strike zone." A line should also be drawn to signify the pitcher's starting point.
                                                    —Jim Leal.

Strike Zone

Age: 9 years and up.
Object: The Canvas Catcher allows a pitcher to face an actual hitter (made of vinyl), and to throw a regulation ball towards a catcher (small net serves as the strike zone).
Equipment: Canvas Catcher and regulation balls.
Rules: Measure out the proper pitching distance (depending on age level). Add an actual indoor pitching mound (baseball) for the older kids. Aim for the "catcher" or boxed strike zone. Use this as a teaching station or competitive game (points for successful throws). Errant tosses should be left alone until the game ends. Always retrieve balls as a group without any more throwing occurring.

Pitcher's Practice

Age: 12 and up.

Object: This activity maps out a preseason pitching and workout schedule.

Equipment: Indoor facility, pitching mounds, batting cage, baseballs, stretch cords, and 3 lb. dumbbells.

Rules: The following is a 6 to 7 week throwing program for 12 pitchers. Set up four groups each with three pitchers. For four practices per week, the groups perform a series of drills. Each week the number of pitches (e.g. per inning) increase to the goal of reaching 6 to 7 innings prior to the first game. The pitchers are grouped 1 to 4. The drills include: Shell Day, Long Toss, Short Bullpen, and Form Throws. Every day the pitchers should stretch, perform calisthenics, and do a warm-up toss. This also includes a series of stretch cord, 3 lb. dumbbell, running, and abdominal exercises.

The Shell Day focuses on actual pitching to a batter. Use a pitch count and strikes versus balls. Week 1 is 15 pitches of regular fastballs equaling that of one inning of work. Each week is an additional 15 pitches adding a different pitch, stretch versus windup, and rest between "innings." Coaches can also film the pitchers (purchase one tape for each person) and hire umpires. Make sure pitchers have been throwing, so they are ready to go for Week 1.

Actual Workout Schedule for Week 1:

Practice #1: Group 1=Shell (15 pitches against actual batter, fastballs, chart or film pitchers in your group, 1 inning, end with 30 minute distance run). Group 2=Long Toss (partner work, 70-feet changeups, bunt coverage and cover first base, end with 20 minute run). Group 3=Short Bullpen (25–35 pitches off a mound, double plays, medicine ball and balance exercises, end with 10 suicide sprints). Group 4=Form Throws (25 pitches off flat ground, target practice, pickoffs, pitchouts, end with pick-ups and 10 sprints).

Practice #2: Group 2=Shell. Group 3=Long Toss. Group 4=Short Bullpen. Group 1=Form Throws.

Practice #3: Group 3=Shell. Group 4=Long Toss. Group 1=Short Bullpen. Group 2=Form Throws.

Practice #4: Group 4=Shell. Group 1=Long Toss. Group 2=Short Bullpen. Group 3=Form Throws.

Week 2: 30 pitches, 15 per inning, four- and two-seam fastballs, sit between innings, 2 innings total). Week 3: 45 pitches, 15 per inning, fastballs and changeups, sit between innings, 3 innings total). Week 4: 60 pitches, 15 per inning, fastballs, changeups and curveballs, sit between innings, 4 innings total). Week 5: 75 pitches, 15 per inning, throw all pitches, work different counts and location, sit between, 5 innings total). Week 6: 90 pitches, 15 per inning, throw all pitches, work live situations, sit between, 6 innings total). Week 7: 100 pitches, 15 per inning, throw all pitches, team scrimmage, sit between, 7 innings total).

Staff Day

Age: 12 and up.
Object: Use a different pitcher for each inning depending on the length of a game or scrimmage.
Equipment: Equipment used in a game.
Rules: Use a different pitcher for each inning. This idea can work great for a scrimmage against another team or an early season match-up when the coach wants to get all of his/her pitchers some action. Make sure the next pitcher is preparing on the side for entry in the upcoming inning. It's best to have a coach directing the bullpen, especially when warming up position players. For 7 innings use 7 pitchers. For 9 innings use 9 pitchers. And for 18 continuous innings (e.g. fall college game) use 9 pitchers at 2 innings each. *Note*: Hitting teams hate facing Staff Day, because they can never get comfortable against a particular pitcher.

Dean the Dummy

Age: 11 years and up.
Object: Learn how to pitch inside and gain confidence in doing so.
Equipment: Baseballs or Incrediballs, *Pitcher's Pal* (mannequin batter), and actual catcher or net to catch the thrown balls.
Rules: Use the *Pitcher's Pal* to help pitchers get used to throwing to

hitters. Pitchers must pitch inside, or command the inner half, (and not be afraid of hitting teammates accidentally) in order to be effective. Great for the bullpen and on Game Day, but it's also a safety tool so hitters aren't getting plunked in practice. The *Pitcher's Pal* allows the pitcher to focus on the catcher's mitt with a simulated batter. This increases accuracy during game situations, because the pitcher is comfortable throwing to a batter in the many positions he/she can take in the batter's box. The dummy is a mobile obstacle which can be placed anywhere in the batter's box as a right or left-handed batter. It's weather-proof and can withstand severe impacts, making it the toughest player on your team. Use it at the field or gym, in the bullpen, backyard, or almost any location you choose to practice the art of pitching. The *Pitcher's Pal* comes with four attachments: head, torso, legs, and square base. Make sure Dean wears a helmet and holds a plastic bat.

T-Drill

Age: 9 years and up.
Object: This is a competitive pitching game.
Equipment: Protective screen or soft toss net, tee, and regulation balls.
Rules: Set up a screen or net just behind home plate. Place a tee, with a ball on top of it, on the plate. Pitchers throw from the rubber. For indoors, use a portable mound and measure off the proper pitching distance according to the age level. Three pitches per person. An instructor should record the points (see below). Declare a winner per station, age group, or up to 25 points, for example. Assign a set pitching order. Attempt to maintain equal rounds of throwing. The on-deck person should be the ball feeder. Pick up the balls as a group. Older players can alternate between the four- and two-seam fastballs as well as the stretch and wind-up.
Scoring includes:
   3 points: Pitch which hits the ball off of the tee.
   2 points: Pitch which hits the tee (pole only).
   1 point: Pitch which hits the screen.
               —Eddie Riley.

Gun It

Age: 11 years and up.

Object: Measure pitching speeds of youngsters, and teach how varying speeds will fool hitters.

Equipment: Rent, purchase, or borrow a radar gun from a local college coach or professional scout. Two brands are *JUGS* and *Bushnell*.

Rules: A quality radar gun can measure the speed of a baseball from 6 to 110mph at 75 feet (e.g. measuring speeds from behind the backstop), and should be accurate to within +/-1mph. For advanced players, use the radar gun when teaching the fastball vs. changeup speed which should differ about 10mph. When throwing the fastball, basic changeup and slider, the arm action (speed of the arm) should be the same. This disguises the different pitches, so a batter can't tell which one is coming. Simply alter the grip and ball placement in the hand. The changing of speeds keep hitters off-stride. The radar gun also reveals velocity. Scouts like to compare speeds for purposes of consistency. During games the gun can be used for measuring velocity each inning, and monitoring whether or not a pitcher is tiring and may be losing something on the fastball. Professional teams have a coach behind the backstop of every game charting each pitch, location (strike or ball), and most likely velocity. Note that velocity is measured at the point of release—not when the ball reaches home plate. Because kids love to throw as hard as they can, make sure everyone is warmed up and loose before trying this activity, and remind them it's not always strength, but precision that determines the success of a pitcher. When using the radar gun at a camp or clinic competition, use velocity readings to track and record a variety of statistics: the speed of pitchers of different ages, the velocity of each pitcher each day, and stats on the fastball vs. changeup numbers. You can also try the *Markwort Speed Sensor Baseball* which measures the speed of the pitch in mph upon impact. This ball is for pitching training only, so do not hit it with a bat or throw it on hard surfaces.

Umpire

Age: 9 years and up.

Object: Pitchers need to learn the strike zone while facing a batter, and get accustomed to game atmosphere.

Equipment: Catching equipment, helmets, bats, balls and gloves.

Rules: During pitching practice with catchers, hitters should stand in the batter's box. No swinging. Catchers call the balls and strikes, and call/frame pitches according to the count. Catchers should call out each pitch, so the hitter can thereby judge velocity, movement, and location of each variety. Then have the hitters try and guess which type of pitch is thrown. Try to alternate between left- and right-handed batters and pitchers. For older players, try rounds of 25 pitches per person. Non-throwers count the number of strikes. Try it as a competition.

Colorful

Age: 11 years and up.

Object: Use color as a way to improve focus and concentration.

Equipment: To fine tune pitching turn a normal home plate into a colorful practice device designed to improve "working the corners." Color the plate into 5 sections: 1) red down the middle, 2–3) yellow on each side of the red, and 4–5) green next to the yellow. Make sure the plate comes with the black edges. For best results aim for the green areas. Remember the four pitching spots: 1) heart of the plate, 2) inner-half, 3) outer-half, and 4) 4 to 6 inches off the plate in and out. You can also make a multi-colored BP tarpaulin for in front of home plate: red (middle), green (left and right of red), and yellow (left and right of green).

Sporting goods companies sell colorful gear to help players develop their focus. Catcher's mitts come with an orange target in the pocket. This helps pitchers "focus on the mitt." Chest protectors also come two-toned in the middle. This aids the advanced pitcher to focus on his/her battery mate, because a good receiver always sets up in the strike zone. Also, invest in the colorful practice baseballs which come with finger placement for the actual pitching grips.

> —Parts of this activity come from Ray Arra and Johanna DiCarlo.

Box

Age: 9 years and up.

Object: Outfielders learn to be accurate on cutoffs.

Equipment: Gloves, Incrediballs, and athletic tape.

Rules: Tape a square target on the gym wall simulating a cutoff throw to an infielder. Stand directly in line with the target. Start off with easy tosses, and progress to game day fashion. Key on pointing the lead leg towards the target, releasing the ball in front of the eyes, and a complete follow through. Balls can be thrown, rolled towards the fielder, or even self-caught. Then line up at an angle; left or right of the target. For competitive purposes, use the following point system: 10 points (balls which hit inside the square), 5 points (balls which hit the tape), and minus 5 points (balls which do not hit the square area at all). The size of the box and the actual distance from the throwers all depends upon the age group.

Biathlon

Age: 9 years and up.

Object: Just as in the winter Olympic sport of target challenges and cross-country skiing, this game combines the talents of throwing and running. The object is to throw balls to designated spots while running against the clock.

Equipment: Stop watch, balls, gloves and bases.

Rules: Scatter balls (one for each person) at the following areas: pitching mound, home plate, first base, second base, third base, shortstop, left field, center field, and right field. Have the instructors or extra players (with gloves on) at home plate, second base, third base, and first base.

At the signal the player runs from each position on the diamond in successive order 1 thru 9: 1 (mound), 2 (plate), 3 (first base), etc. At Number 1, throw to the catcher. At Number 2, throw to second base. At Number 3, throw to third base. At Numbers 4-5-6, throw to first base. At Number 7, throw to home plate. At Number 8, throw to second base. And at Number 9, throw to third base.

Younger kids can throw to second base from the outfield positions. Time limits can vary for the age groups. Make sure the kids run or jog from station to station. An umpire tallies the scores, and has the right to award points even after errors by a receiver. No points are allowed for balls which roll to the target, or draw the receivers away from the bag.

Scoring includes:

3 points: Perfect throw to the receiver.

2 points: Throw which is bounced, picked, or scooped by the receiver.

1 point: Throw which moves the receiver left or right of the base.

Rebound

Age: 9 years and up.

Object: Use the following indoor activities for both infielders and outfielders.

Equipment: Incrediballs and gloves.

Rules: For a long toss drill, set the kids up in pairs across from each other along the short way of the gym. Have the receiver facing the opposite wall. One person fires the ball high against the cement wall (use the crow-hop). The receiver catches the ball, hustles back to his/her wall, and then throws across the gym. Repeat the exercise back and forth with each person running and throwing.

For a drill to work on grip, set the kids up in one long line facing a gym wall and about 7 to 10 feet away. Throw about half-speed. Work on getting the proper grip before each throw. Do about 25 to 50 of these every day.

Heave-Ho

Age: 7 years and up.

Object: This game emphasizes throwing to different spots in the diamond.

Equipment: Anything used for a real game (no bats).

Rules: Make two teams. Treat this as a regular game except the batter catches the ball from the pitcher (use gloves). The batter then throws the ball anywhere into the field of play. A foul ball is an out. A batter is also out if he/she misses or drops the pitch (must be a strike for this to occur). Batters have three seconds in which to throw. No bunting.

Throw Ball

Age: 7 years and up.

Object: Anything used for a real game (no bats).

Equipment: Gloves, balls and bases.

Rules: Make two teams, and set up a regulation diamond. The defensive team should play separate positions with one person at each bag. The hitting team should make a lineup and bat accordingly. Treat this as a regular game except the batter catches the ball from the pitcher (use gloves). The batter then throws the ball anywhere into the field of play. The goal is to run to first base and then back home before the fielders can retrieve the ball and tag either first, second, or third base. If successful a run is scored. Outs include the following: ball is brought to a base before the runner reaches home, any foul ball, or a fly ball caught in the air. A batter is also out if he/she misses or drops the pitch (must be a strike for this to occur). Batters have three seconds in which to throw. The bunt is allowed.

—Marilyn Gould, Playground Sports (New York:
Lothrop, Lee & Shepard, 1978).

Punch Ball

Age: 7 years and up.

Object: Practice running bases and home fielding skills.

Equipment: Four bases of any kind plus a kick ball.

Rules: "Rules are similar to that for baseball except there is no pitcher or catcher, stealing bases and bunting are not allowed, and there are no strikes, so a miss or a foul equals an out. When up to bat, the plays toss the ball in the air or bounces it and then punches it. If a runner is heading toward home plate and the outfielder throws the ball to home plate before the runner arrives there, he is out. Play seven or nine innings."

—Spaldeen Games, www.spaldeen.com.

Beat Ball

Age: 8 to 12 years old.

Object: Throwing accuracy and running speed all come into play in this game.

Equipment: Bases, gloves, helmets and Incrediballs.

Rules: Make two teams with about seven kids on each. One team runs the bases.

The other team places a person near each infield base. Include a pitcher and catcher. Extra fielders can back up, or rotate into the action after each throw. Play begins with the pitcher throwing the ball to the catcher who then throws to the first baseman. This person must tag the base with their foot before throwing to the second baseman, and so on, until the ball reaches home plate.

Simultaneously, the first runner, who starts at first base, sprints around the bases in an effort to "beat" the ball home. If successful, a run is scored; otherwise, an out is called. After three outs, the teams change positions and the game continues. For safety purposes, fielders should throw "inside" or "outside" of the runner.

—Keg Wheeler and Otto H. Spilker, *Physical Education Curriculum Activities Kit* (New York: Parker Publishing Company, 1991).

Wall Ball

Age: 6 years and up.

Object: Learn the different throwing release points according to varying distances and heights.

Equipment: Balls and cones.

Rules: Arrange equal throwing stations about 15 to 20 feet away from
the backstop. Everyone must stand behind their designated cone.
Place the balls near each cone. Use the various levels on the backstop as different target areas. Either use three throws per player, or
rotate from cone to cone after each throw. Kids can use the crow-
hop as part of their toss. Only collect the balls until after everyone
has gone. Increase the distances after several successful throws by
the group. Either use 2 to 3 groups for one side of the backstop or
4 to 5 groups when using both sides.

German Baseball

Age: 6 years and up.

Object: This game works on throwing accuracy.

Equipment: Tee, Nerf ball or kickball, bat and cones.

Rules: Tell the group that a long time ago Germans played a version
of baseball using a large knackwurst (bat) and hard-boiled onion
(ball). Start with one team in the field, and the other standing
against a wall in their batting order. The fielding team divides in
half, and forms two lines facing each other about 20 to 30 feet
apart. Cones are 5 to 10 feet apart, and should equal the number
of players on each side of the playing area. Home plate is at one
end, and second base (cone) is in the center of the far end.

The pitcher, standing in the middle between the cones, can
either roll (kicking) or throw (hitting) the ball depending on age
levels. After contact the hitter runs around second base and back
to home plate. The fielders attempt to either catch or retrieve the
ball, and get the runner out by hitting him/her below the waist
with it.

If the runner is successful in reaching home plate without being
hit by the ball, a run is scored, and the next batter runs to second

base. The runners must tag each other behind home plate before beginning to run. Keep going until a runner is hit by the ball. When an out is recorded, the next person in line is up. After the third out, the batting order continues from that spot the next inning. A person can only throw the ball from behind his/her designated cone (same for each inning). The group can pass/throw the ball to another team member for a better shot at the runner. Any stray ball can only be retrieved by the closest defensive person. Use a manual scoreboard to keep track of the runs.

−Kathy Cardillo.

Court Ball

Age: 9 years and up.

Object: Play an exciting and competitive throwing game emphasizing accuracy, quick release, and communication between fielders.

Equipment: Tennis balls and gloves.

Rules: Play on a tennis court with a net separating the two sides. Apply actual tennis rules with serves, scoring, etc. Teams of 4 on each side. Two set up in the front boxes, and two set up at the back lines. The right to serve, receive, choose your side, or give the opponent these choices is decided by a coin toss. Remember that serves have to land in the opposite cross-court. The server shall not throw until the receiver is ready (e.g. if an attempt is made to return the server's ball). Serves must be overhand. Fielders can throw overhand, sidearm, or flip the ball. After the serve is successful you don't have to wait for the ball to bounce on the ground. The players in front of the server (both boxes) should vacate their area until the serve is successful whereupon both players can return to their fielding spots (e.g. the receiver gets a clear view of the serve). The server stands behind the baseline on the deuce court within the boundaries of the doubles sideline. All even points are played from the deuce court and odd number points played from the advantage court. Serves are made from the deuce court to the opponents' service box on the deuce court. Advantage court to advantage box. If the server misses the target twice, a point is lost. If the ball hits the net and goes in the correct service box, another serve is granted.

If the server steps on the baseline before contact is made, the serve is deemed a fault. The receiver or fielder has 1 second to throw or for one to set his/her feet (decide ruling before playing). You cannot throw at the body of a person (e.g. no close range body shots). No diving. Sportsmanship counts especially when balls are close to the lines.

The receiver can stand where he/she likes, but must let the ball bounce in the service box. The server always calls his/her score first. If the server wins the first point, he/she gets a score of 15. Scoring is done like a clock. Love means zero in tennis. The second point is called 30. The third point is called 40, and the game is won when the score goes back to love. If the score is 40–40 (deuce), one side must win by two points. Advantage-In means if the server wins the next point, he/she wins the game. Advantage-Out means the receiver has a chance to win the game on the next point. Thus, LOVE 15–30–40.

After the game, the opponents serve. Games equal 1. The first to win 6 games, by two, wins the set. First service is switched after each set. The first to win 3 sets (doubles format) wins the match. If the score is 6–6, a tie-breaker is played. This is scored by one's. The first team to score 7 points winning by two wins the set. The tiebreaker continues until one side wins by two. Hence, Game-Set-Match. If the ball goes into the net, or outside the boundaries of the court (doubles play the entire space), the team that threw the ball loses the point. If the ball hits the net during the point and goes into the opponents court, the ball is in play. A team loses the point if he/she touches the net, drops his/her glove while fielding a ball, bounces the ball over the net, the ball touches a teammate, or deliberately tries to distract the opponent (e.g. yelling or fake tosses). A let is called during the point if a ball rolls on the court or there's a distraction from someone besides the players on the court. A ball that lands on the line is good. If players serve out of turn or serve to the wrong person or court, the point or game will stand and order will be resumed following the point or game.

Hot Potato

Age: 9 years and up.

Object: This is a great game for improving throwing technique; especially the double play pivot.

Equipment: Gloves and balls for everyone; can also use wooden infield paddles with tennis balls or Incrediballs.

Rules: Arrange groups of two in throwing lines but in close proximity to each other. Demonstrate the three-quarter's arm angle, and receiving the ball with an open glove. Stand in an athletic position ready to receive the toss. Start with the balls on one side. Play quick catch. Time the groups for 1 to 2 minutes or to 30 points. Every catch equals one point for the group (count silently). For a missed throw the ball must be retrieved, and only thrown again until that person gets back to their original spot. After each round, rotate one group to the left in order to switch partners. Players can also throw bare-handed with tennis balls.

Twenty-One

Age: 9 years and up.

Object: Throw the ball as accurately as possible.

Equipment: Gloves and balls for everyone.

Rules: Partners should stand 60 to 90 feet apart depending on the skill/ age level. Throw like a pitcher or fielder (crow-hop for outfielders). Aim for the head, chest, or belt of your partner. This is the ideal throwing location, because it is easier to handle at those spots. The receiver (umpire) verbally calls out the score for that particular throw plus the total score for his/her opponent. The fielder can only move his/her feet for errant throws (in this case no points are awarded). The first person to 21 wins. A player must win by two points for the game to end.

Scoring includes:

   3 points: Any ball caught in the chest area.

   2 points: Any ball caught in the area of the head or belt.

   1 point: Any ball caught left or right of the receiver (in the vicinity of the midsection).

Radar

Age: 9 years and up.

Object: After a throwing warm-up, play a simple game done between partners. The object is to gain points by throwing the ball to a specific area. Try "Radar" as a test of throwing accuracy.

Equipment: Balls and gloves.

Rules: Arrange partners in throwing lines some distance apart according to the age level. The partner without the ball should place his/her glove at a particular location in the "ideal throwing zones" of either the head, shoulders, chest or belt. The thrower must then attempt to throw the ball to that exact spot to earn a point. The receiver's glove cannot move after it has been set. If the thrower fails to hit the target, the receiver must obviously catch the ball anyway. It would then be this person's time to throw. Each successful toss equals one point each. Play to 10 points.

—Dave Smith and Bob Casaceli.

Ultimate Throw & Catch

Age: 8 years and up.

Object: This competitive game teaches throwing accuracy, teamwork and quickness.

Equipment: Incrediball, gloves, and colored vests.

Rules: Make two distinct teams. Designate playing boundaries similar to a game of "Ultimate Frisbee." While playing outside on a diamond, name the outfield foul lines as the "touchdown areas." Kids can play anywhere but only on the outfield grass, for example. The goal is to complete a series of throws to teammates, and then reach the other foul line.

One team starts with the ball. Attempt to make accurate throws. You cannot throw underhand. Defenders must stand at least three feet away, and cannot touch anyone from the opposing team. Receivers can only take 2 or 3 steps after a successful catch. Upon receiving the ball, throwers must make a toss within five seconds or else a turnover is called. Make short tosses or long ones. After a dropped or missed throw, the ball goes to the other team. One point is awarded for every successful throw caught beyond the foul line. After a "touchdown," the "losing" team should walk to the other end line. The next game should begin with a "throw-off" to the other team. Play to 10 points.

—Dave Smith and Bob Casaceli.

Wig the Bat

Age: 8 years and up (adjust to skill level).

Object: This high-energy game teaches kids to take their time before throwing, the correct grip, accuracy, and a proper follow through.

Equipment: Two Incrediballs (baseball-size), four bats, and two bases.

Rules: "Wig the Bat" works better outside, but use your imagination for an indoor game. The instructor should make two groups with equal strong and weak throwers. Put each base in front of and beside the pitching mound. Align the teams behind each base. Set the lower squared-off sections of the chain-link fence backstop as the throwing targets. In each section hang two bats out from the fence. At the drop of the hat from the instructor, the first person in line fires the ball at the backstop. After a throw, the umpire yells out points or no points (see below). Every throw must occur from behind the base. No points are awarded for any illegal tosses.

The thrower must retrieve his/her ball and toss it back to the next person in line, who again throws the ball, and so on. This person should get a good grip on the ball and focus on their target. For safety reasons align the teams away from the throwing lanes. Before throwing make sure no one from the other team is in your way. After a turn go to the end of the line. Overthrows or poor throws will cause his/her team to fall behind. These types of throws cannot be stopped or blocked by anyone else besides the next thrower in line.

Two instructors (umpires) should keep track of scoring by verbally calling out points and violations (see below) for each team. The first team to reach 40 points is the winner. After each game teams should switch sides. The deciding game of a series is called a "Wig-Off." At camp try a team competition which lasts all week. If the games go quickly, lengthen them to 50 or 60 points. Switch the better players from time to time as well. Players should cheer for their own team. Include helmets, more bats, and other equipment per side if desired (add scores for balls which hit multiple pieces of equipment). The scoring is as follows:

Points:

> Game Over: Ball hits both bats and both fall to the ground.
> 15: Ball lodges in the fence; called a "Stucky."
> 10: Ball hits both bats, and one bat falls to the ground.
> 5: Ball hits one bat, and it falls to the ground.
> 3: Ball hits a bat, but it does not fall to the ground.
> 2: Ball hits the designated throwing area.
> 2: Ball wedges in the target area then falls out; called "False Wiggage."
> 1: Ball hits the pipes around the designated throwing square.

Minus Points:

> -15: A "Stucky" in the target area of the opposing team.
> - 5: Player steps over the throwing boundary.
> - 2: Ball hits another team's throwing section.
> - 1: Ball hits the fenced section above or to the side of the target area.

No Points:

> Any ball which hits the ground first, or completely misses the backstop.

Violations:

> Certain penalties can result where an umpire tosses or "hoists" the ball into the outfield, called a "Harvey Hoistington." That player must run after it, and return to line while the other team continues on. Violations include illegal touching or interference with another team's ball, or arguing with an umpire's call.
>
>   —Dave Smith and Bob Casaceli.

Wig the Coach

Age: 7 to 10 years old.

Object: Kids aim a throw at an instructor dressed in catcher's equipment.

Equipment: Tennis balls or Incrediballs, catcher's equipment, protective cup, work boots, and jackets.

Rules: A brave adult should dress in full catcher's equipment along with added bulk such as sweatpants, jackets, and work boots. The catcher should watch the flight of the ball, and give the pitcher a target with his/her glove. Kids start at the pitching mound with the catcher standing or crouching behind home plate. Points are only awarded according to balls which *hit* the catcher. The instructor cannot move away from the throw, but should tilt his/her head down slightly. Tally up the points until someone reaches 30. After each throw return to the end of the line.

Scoring includes:

    15 points: Ball hits the mask; called "Wig the Coach."

    10 points: Ball hits the glove.

     7 points: Ball hits the arm.

     5 points: Ball hits the chest protector.

     3 points: Ball hits the shin pads.

     1 point: Ball hits the feet.

                —Dave Smith and Bob Casaceli.

Wig the Cone

Age: 8 years and up.

Object: Teach outfielders about the importance of strong, accurate, and even bounced throws to cutoff people.

Equipment: Balls, gloves, bat and cones.

Rules: Place a cone or barrel at first base, second base, third base, and home plate. Set up fielders at the three outfield positions. The instructor should hit grounders and fly balls from home plate. After a catch, fielders must attempt to make strong throws to each of the targets. Try two throws for each person to each base. Keep the rotation going until someone reaches 20 points.

Scoring includes:

    5 points: Throws which land in (barrel) or knock the target over (cone).

    3 points: Throws which hit the target on the fly.

    2 points: Throws which one-hop the target.

    1 point: Throws which roll and hit the target.

The instructor can also apply a similar game for catchers throwing to either first, second, or third base.

                —Dave Smith and Bob Casaceli.

Three-Two-One

Age: 7 years and up.
Object: This game stresses the importance of crisp, accurate throws around the infield.
Equipment: Bases, balls, bats and helmets.
Rules: Make two teams, and assign a batting order to each. The offensive team hits soft toss from home plate. The defensive team aligns its players around the field with only one person at the infield positions. After contact, the hitter should run around the bases and touch as many bases as possible. For those truly epic blasts, the runner should continue on even after touching home plate. The offensive team should count out loud for each base touched (points).

The ball must be thrown either from third base to second base to first base and to home plate, or from first to second to third and to home. The runner stops after the last successful throw. Keep running if there is an overthrow. Depending upon the location of a hit to the outfield, the defensive team must make the most logical toss to the infielders for the sequence to start. Encourage verbal calls (base number) before making a throw. Fielders should be aware of the runner, and make throws around/away from them. Switch defensive positions each inning. A variation of this game may include tosses to every person on the field.
—Cindy Harrington.

Slow-Pitch Softball

Age: 8 years and up.
Object: This is the traditional game played in physical education classes.
Equipment: Anything used for a real game.
Rules: The major differences between regular softball and "Slow-Pitch Softball" lie in the pitching. The pitch must be a slow toss with an arc of at least six feet and not more than 12 feet from the ground. Any other pitch is illegal and thus called a ball. This call is determined by the umpire. Use 10 fielders instead of nine. This roving fielder should stand in "short field" between the infield and outfield. The batter must take a full swing at the pitch. No bunting or chop-

ping at the ball. If hit by a pitch, a ball is called and the batter continues to hit. Runners must wait until the pitch has crossed home plate. No bunting, leading or stealing. Use the same rules, balls, strikes, outs, and runs as in regular softball.

Missile

Age: 6 years and up.

Object: To teach proper throwing technique to youngsters, "Missile" is the way to go.

Equipment: Nerf balls of every size and shape.

Rules: Make two teams. Each person must stay on their own side of a basketball court. Put the balls inside the tip-off circle. At the starting signal, run and get the balls. Throw the ball overhand at kids on the opposite side. Aim below the shoulders. Once hit, join the other team. Issue penalties (i.e. push-ups) to anyone who throws sidearm. Throws which hit kids in the head do not count. Keep playing until everyone is on a single team. Another version is to play "Freeze Tag." Anyone hit by the ball has to "freeze." The only way to become "unfrozen" is for a teammate to safely tag you. Use the entire gym for this game.

Ball Tag

Age: 6 years and up.

Object: Teach proper throwing technique with an added bonus of trying to elude the "It" people.

Equipment: Enough Nerf balls to equal half the number of people in the group.

Rules: Start by issuing restricted boundaries. Designate 2 to 3 people to be "It." To be immune from a tag, a player must be holding a ball. You can only have one ball at a time, and a ball cannot be thrown at the same person twice in succession. "It" people must either throw the ball overhand or actually tag the person. Those hit or tagged by the ball thus become "It" people.

Hose Master

Age: 10 years and up.

Object: This drill teaches proper throwing technique from the outfield and includes a baserunning tagging up exercise.

Equipment: Balls, gloves, bases and helmets.

Rules: First explain the crow-hop and throwing technique to the outfielders as well as how to properly tag up at third base on a fly ball to the outfield. Form three groups (outfielders, runners and catchers). Make sure base runners wear helmets. The outfield group should be arranged at standard playing distance in left, center, and right field. The coach will toss balls in the air from behind the pitching mound to a particular outfielder. The goal is for the outfielder to throw the runner out at home plate. Runners cannot advance until a catch is made in the outfield. Two points are awarded for an out (to the outfielder who threw the ball), and two points for being safe (to the runner who scored on the throw). The catchers group should have an "on-deck person" directing any needed slides or to stand up. Rotate runners, outfielders and catchers, so everyone gets an equal number of turns. No cut-off people. See who has the "Best Hose" on the team.

                                    —Dave Smith.

Hit the Bat

Age: 9 years and up.

Object: Fielders try to make accurate throws to the plate.

Equipment: Balls, bats and gloves.

Rules: Arrange players throughout the diamond, including a catcher (optional), with one batter and a pitcher. Stay up until contact is made. After a catch that fielder throws the ball towards the batter. The bat should be placed on the ground and facing the fielder. In order to throw all balls must be fielded cleanly. After a fly ball catch, you can take 10 steps in. After a ground ball catch, you can take five steps in. Thus, the longer the hit the more difficult the throw. The fielder gets to hit if the throw bounces directly over, or hits the bat. With a small group, have the batter hit the ball out of his/her hand. Then pick up a glove and receive the throw to home plate.

Pyramid

Age: 9 years and up.
Object: Fielders can test their throwing accuracy.
Equipment: Tee, ball, numerous bats, and gloves.
Rules: Put players at every position. Stand a series of bats (form of a pyramid) at home plate. A player hits a ball off of a tee in front of home plate. The person who fields/catches the ball can take 1 to 2 steps before throwing the ball towards the pyramid. If the pyramid falls, that player hits next. If not, the original batter hits until someone knocks the pyramid over.

Rain Delay

Age: 11 years and up.
Object: Try to pass the time between rain drops.
Equipment: General baseball gear.
Rules: The following are some activities to perform during a rain delay. First, *Ball Mail*. Take an old ball and write a message on it. Toss it to the other team's dugout. Once received that team has to "answer the mail." Throw it back each time with a different "letter." Try messages, trivia, or whatever makes you laugh. Second, *Talk Show Fungo*. One of the more talkative kids or coaches on the team can set up their own "talk show" using a fungo or bat as the microphone. Interview the shy kid. Imitate a coach. Analyze the status of your current team or favorite big league club. Third, *Bucket Stomp*. Pound away on the buckets you use to house the baseballs. Use bats as "drumsticks." Get the rhythm and noise down to a beat. Fourth, *Upside Down Uniform*. You really need a character to pull this one off. With help from a teammate have a player dress up in the gym or concession shack. Basically switch up the clothes from top to bottom. Slip uniform pants over the arms with the zipper slightly open so the person can see. Cleats, socks, and stirrups go over the hands. Pull the uniform top up over your legs, so you're walking around in bare feet. Then without warning the mystery person should stumble out into full view of both teams. It appears that the person is walking on their hands. Fifth, *Ball Unravel*. Take an old ball and unwind it down to the core. Examine what actu-

ally makes up a baseball. And if you want to save those balls from the "Wet Ball Cemetery," purchase some *Ball Dry*. The granules kit can dry dozens of balls before being saturated, and can be reactivated for reuse. The moisture indicators are blue when dry and turn pink when saturated. For other ideas see the "Indoor Schedule" in Chapter 1.

Dart Baseball

Age: 6 years and up.
Object: Practice your aim using darts.
Equipment: Piece of beaver board, different colors of paint, and darts for both teams.
Rules: Draw the illustrated layout on a piece of beaver board at least 36 inches square. The home run bull's-eye circle should be 3 inches in diameter and painted red. Paint the other areas in contrasting colors. Hang the board so that the bull's-eye is at about eye level of the shortest player. Any number of persons may play divided into two teams. Each in his/her turn "at bat" throws darts from a distance of 15 feet until he/she either gets on base or is put out. If a dart fails to hit the board or stick in it, it is scored as an out. A dart that sticks directly on a line does not count. It's important that darts should never be thrown when anyone is in front of the throwing line. Play follows that of regular baseball, one team continuing to throw in each inning until it has made three outs. In case of a hit, any base runners advance an equal number of bases. If "sacrifice" is thrown, it is an out; but, if it isn't the third out, any base runners advance one base each. "DP," or double play, puts out both the batter and the most advanced runner; other runners advance one base. To keep track of the runners on bases, you might make or adapt a peg board, or use the corners of a checkerboard with checkers for runners.
—Jack Redford.

Baseball Gags

Age: 14 years and up.
Object: To blow off steam.

Rules: "Hot Foots" is where a teammate's shoelaces are set on fire in the dugout. Put a bubble gum bubble on top of someone's hat. For the player who takes the game too seriously, slap some eye black around the inside visor of his/her hat. Give a shaving cream pie in the face to someone getting interviewed by the media. Put shot-puts in the freshmen player's travel bags. On the plane ride to Florida have the rookies wear funky out of style ties purchased at the local Salvation Army. And for that unsuspecting youngster, try the Abbott and Costello "Who's on First?" routine. "Who" plays first. "What" plays second. "I Don't Know" plays third. "Why" is in left field. "Because" is in center. "Today" is catching. "Tomorrow" is pitching, and "I Don't Care" plays shortstop.

Baseball Quizzes

Age: 8 years and up.

Object: Whether on a rainy day or simply for the fun of it, this is a great game to help kids learn about the baseball greats.

Equipment: Chalkboard, chalk and eraser.

Rules: Challenge the kids to ask and answer a variety of questions about their favorite players. They can write their ideas and answers on the board. Here are a few to get them started. Who were some stars who played for only one team? Name as many Hall of Famers as you can according to position. Match up legends and their nicknames. Here's a sample:

2006 All-Stars: American League Starters: P Kenny Rogers (Tigers), C Ivan Rodriguez (Tigers), 1B David Ortiz (Red Sox), 2B Mark Loretta (Red Sox), 3B Alex Rodriguez (Yankees), SS Derek Jeter (Yankees), OF Vladimir Guerrero (Angels), OF Ichiro Suzuki (Mariners), OF Vernon Wells (Blue Jays). National League Starters: P Brad Penny (Dodgers), C Paul Lo Duca (Mets), 1B Albert Pujols (Cardinals), 2B Chase Utley (Phillies), 3B David Wright (Mets), SS Edgar Renteria (Braves), OF Jason Bay (Pirates), OF Carlos Beltran (Mets), OF Alfonso Soriano (Nationals).

Teams Played For: Reggie Jackson (Kansas City and Oakland A's, Baltimore Orioles, New York Yankees, California Angles), Babe

Ruth (Boston Red Sox and Braves, New York Yankees), Steve Carlton (St. Louis Cardinals, Philadelphia Phillies, San Francisco Giants, Chicago White Sox, Cleveland Indians, Minnesota Twins), Nolan Ryan (New York Mets, California Angels, Houston Astros, Texas Rangers), Frank Robinson (Cincinnati Reds, Baltimore Orioles, Los Angeles Dodgers, California Angels, Cleveland Indians).

Players Synonymous with One Team: Cal Ripken Jr. (Orioles), Ted Williams (Red Sox), Bob Feller (Indians), Al Kaline (Tigers), George Brett (Royals), Robin Yount (Brewers), Mickey Mantle (Yankees), Edgar Martinez (Mariners), Luke Appling (White Sox), Tony Oliva (Twins), Rocco Baldelli (Devil Rays), Ernie Banks (Cubs), Johnny Bench (Reds), Mike Schmidt (Phillies), Mel Ott (Giants), Todd Helton (Rockies), Stan Musial (Cardinals), Roberto Clemente (Pirates), Chipper Jones (Braves), Tony Gwynn (Padres), Jackie Robinson (Dodgers), Walter Johnson (Senators).

Notable Hall of Famers: P (Christy Mathewson, Sandy Koufax, Bob Gibson, Cy Young, Walter Johnson, Lefty Grove), C (Yogi Berra, Roy Campanella, Mickey Cochrane, Carlton Fisk, Johnny Bench), 1B (Lou Gehrig, Jimmie Foxx, Willie McCovey, Hank Greenberg, Willie Stargell), 2B (Joe Morgan, Bobby Doerr, Rogers Hornsby, Nap Lajoie, Jackie Robinson), SS (Ozzie Smith, Pee Wee Reese, Honus Wagner, Ernie Banks, Joe Cronin), 3B (Eddie Mathews, Mike Schmidt, Brooks Robinson, Pie Traynor, Frank Baker), OF (Ty Cobb, Hank Aaron, Willie Mays, Joe DiMaggio, Carl Yastrzemski, Tris Speaker).

Nicknames: Say Hey Kid (Willie Mays), Charlie Hustle (Pete Rose), Pudge (Carlton Fisk), Big Train (Walter Johnson), Iron Horse (Lou Gehrig), Rocket (Roger Clemens), Georgia Peach (Ty Cobb), Splendid Splinter (Ted Williams), Mr. Cub (Ernie Banks), Mr. October (Reggie Jackson), The Beast (Jimmie Foxx), Great Bambino (Babe Ruth), Shoeless (Joe Jackson).

Game Attractions

Age: 12 years and up.
Object: These minor league baseball ideas can promote individual teams and bring fans to the games.

Pre-game: Ask volunteers to sing the National Anthem and be guest PA announcers. Field of Dreams (be on the field with the players during the anthem, run the bases, and throw on the field after a game). Celebratory first pitches (former coaches, politicians, dignitaries). Kids Club (special membership and awards). Hire a DJ complete with music, speakers, and a microphone. Bobble Head Day. Giveaways (team photos and posters, pocket schedules, magnets, seat cushions, Homer Hankies, Tomahawk Chops, or Thunder Sticks). Free kids clinic. Specialty events focusing on the team name (e.g. Huskies=bring in trained dogs to deliver the game balls to the umpire). Nationality Night (Italian, Irish, Swedish). Look a Like or Dress-up Days (Elvis, Halloween, 1970s, baseball uniforms). Hair Days (mullets, mustaches, beards). Fan Appreciation Day, family picnic spots, and birthday parties. Autographed team trading cards. Reunion Celebrations (e.g. 1987 State Champs). *Between innings*: Potato sack races. Race the mascot around the bases. Water balloon soft toss smash. Pie eating contest. Close range target tosses. Toss free T-shirts and bags of peanuts to the fans. Announce birthdays. Let's Make a Deal contest. Flying Fowl (use a net to catch a rubber chicken shot from a giant sling shot). Dizzy Bat Race. Kid's play area (Simon Says, caricaturist, radar ball tosses). *Post-game*: Dirtiest car in the parking lot gets a free car wash. Corporate sponsorships (ADs on outfield wall), giveaways, and gift certificates. Launch a Ball contest ($1 for each tennis ball, once game ends toss from stands, if your numbered ball lands closest to second base you win a prize). 50/50 raffle. Fireworks or a post-game concert. For other ideas read *Fun is Good* by Mike Veeck.

Closing Words

I'd walk through hell in a gasoline suit to keep playing baseball. —*Pete Rose*

Several "gifts to the game" have made baseball and softball ever so unique and special, the likes of which include the Little League World Series, 60-feet-six-inches, Cape Cod Summer League, pine tar, 7th inning stretch, Babe Ruth, the idea of the sacrifice bunt, Boys of Summer, the movie "Field of Dreams," all-day softball tournaments, and the Wiffle ball.

In some cases, kids may be experiencing baseball or softball for the very first time. Turn them onto the sports. One way to accomplish this is to communicate through "the lingo." Save the big words for the thesaurus. Use the following "dictionary" as a way to turn key themes into catch phrases.

It's no wonder that major leaguers are sometimes called adults playing a child's game. The terminology is totally original. Words and phrases are familiar yet poignant. Learn, know, and cherish them.

The Field—Diamond, Park, Yard: Field. *Band Box, Homer Dome, Launching Pad:* Hitter's ballpark. *Dish:* Home plate. *Rubber:* Slab on mound which pitcher stands on. *Hill:* Mound. *Sack, Bag:* Base. *Pit:* Batter's box. *Left/Right Side:* Third base-shortstop/second base-first base. *Inside/Outside:* Closer to mound/away from mound. *Hole:* Area between infielders. *Corners:* Edges of plate, or first or third base. *Lip:* Edges of infield. *Gaps:* Left or right center. *Triangle:* Deep center. *No Man's Land:* Territory beyond outfielders. *Warning Track:* Sandy area along outfield fence.

Hitting—Swinger: Batter. *Rip, Cut:* A swing. *Frozen Rope, Liner, Laser Beam, Missile, Bullet, Shot, Screamer, Seed, Pea, On the Button* or *Nose:* Hard hit. *Crushed, Jacked, Crunched, Hammered, Smashed, Muckled, Spanked, Tattooed, Laced, Dented, Postmarked:* Deep drive. *Pop:* Power. *Air Raid, Blitz:* Multiple hits. *Work the Pitcher:* Ability to extend count. *Battle, Stay Alive, Get Money's Worth, Put Another Quarter In:* Numerous foul ball swings. *English:* Rotation of ball after contact. *Dinger, Going Yard* or *Deep, Bomb, Round-Tripper, Put Into Orbit, Tater, Moon Shot:* Home run. *Grand Slam:* Bases-loaded homer. *Trot:* Home run jog. *Walk-Off:* Game-ending hit. *Crooked Number:* Multiple runs. *Switch Hitter:* Can bat from both sides of plate. *Slugger, Bull, Guerilla, Masher:* Power hitter. *Pull, Turn On It:* Hitting inside pitch. *Bad Ball, Hacker, Free Swinger:* Swings at anything. *Dead Red:* Looking fastball. *Pinch Hitter:* Substitute batter. *DH:* Non-fielding starter. *All-Fields Hitter:* Few weaknesses. *Spray Hitter:* Hitting pitch according to location. *Table Setter:* Lead-off hitter. *Cleanup:* Fourth batter. *Double Lead-Off:* Ninth batter.

On-Deck: Next to bat. *In the Hole:* Third hitter in order. *Heart of Order:* Best hitters. *BP, Beeps:* Pre-game hitting. *Lightning Round:* Swings at end of BP. *Triple Crown:* Leader in batting average, RBI and homers. *Silver Slugger:* Batting champion. *Scoring Position:* Runner on second or third base. *On-Base Percentage:* Reaching safely according to plate appearances. *Slugging Average:* Ratio of total bases to at-bats. *Fielder's Choice:* Force out on bases. *Walk, Free Pass:* Base on balls. *Bagger, Light the Lamp:* Base hit. *Ground Rule Double:* Fair ball which bounces out of play. *Cycle:* Single, double, triple, and home run in same game. *Watermelon, Balloon:* Appearance of ball during success. *Down the Pipe, Heart,* or *Broadway:* Pitch down middle of plate. *Back Through Box, Spin a Cap:* Hit going up middle. *Slice:* Angular movement to hit. *Bloop and a Blast:* Strategy against tough pitcher. *Texas Leaguer, Flare, Chink, Gork, Dink, Cheapy:* Soft base hit. *Seeing Eye, Bleeder:* Base hit just out of infielder's reach. *Nubber, Dribbler, Cue* or *Squib Shot:* Ball hit off end of bat. *Chopper:* Bouncing ground ball. *Dead Ball Era:* Early 1900s when pitching dominated.

Hitting Techniques—Stance: Position before swinging either even, closed or open. *Pigeon-Toed:* Toes pointed inward in stance. *Stride:* Motion of front foot towards pitcher. *Sacrifice, Drag, Squeeze:* Bunt plays. *Sac Fly:* Fly ball which scores tagging runner. *Hit-and-Run, Bunt-and-Run, Hit-Behind-Runner, Slash:* Offensive plays. *Bat Control:* Hitting ability. *Bat Speed:* A quick bat. *Slap, Punch-and-Judy:* Contact hitter. *Take One for Team, Wear It, Plunked, Drilled:* Hit by pitch. *Hang In, Hold Ground:* Reaction to inside pitch. *Guarding* or *Crowding the Dish:* Protecting with two-strikes. *Jackknife:* Body position while avoiding close inside pitch. *Green/Red Light:* Swing away/take sign. *Guess:* Pre-determined notion about pitch. *Read:* Watching flight of ball. *Going with Pitch, Plate Coverage:* Hitting according to location. *Compact, Short Swing:* Fundamentally sound. *Inside Out:* Taking inside pitch to opposite field. *Baltimore Chop:* Hit bouncing off home plate. *Crack of the Bat:* Running on contact with two outs. *Protect Runner, Swing Through:* Offering at pitch on steal play. *Steal Runs:* Aggressive baserunning. *Dry, Air Swing:* Swinging with no ball present. *Dig In:* Foundation for stance. *Choke and Poke:* Two-strike swing. *Attack, Ready, Launching Positions:* Area for hands in stance. *Happy Feet:* Tapping of front foot in stance. *Lock & Load:* Hitting prep. *Coil, Cock, Trigger:* Action before swing. *Step on Thin Ice:* Stride of front foot. *Mash the Bug:* Turning on front foot. *Weight Shift:* Movement into pitch. *Fire, Throw Hands:* Direction of hands to pitch. *Get on Top:* Swinging down. *Name on It, In Your Wheelhouse* or *Shoebox:* Favorite pitch. *Nice Peepers:* Knowledge of strike zone. *Sweet Spot, Meat:* Best hitting area near end of bat. *Impact, Hitting Zone:* Area just in front of plate. *Flat Bat:* Level swing. *Palm-Up Palm-Down:* Hands on contact. *L-to-I:* Full lead-arm extension. *Ike-to-Mike:* Shoulder-to-shoulder. *Magician:* Top-hand released swing. *V:* Formation of bat and lead-arm in one-handed follow through.

Hitting Flaws—Statue: Stiff stance. *Flat-Footed:* Not on the balls of the feet. *Hitch:* Flaw with hands. *Chicken wing:* Lifting of front arm in swing. *Step in Bucket, Caviat:* Hitter steps away from pitcher. *Bat Wrap:* Bat improperly goes in front of head. *Check Swing:* Indecisive half-swing. *Uppercut, Loopy:* Swinging under ball. *Long Swing:* Slow developing swing. *Buckle:* Bending on curveball. *Jumpy:* Too aggressive. *Wave:* Swing and miss. *Hat Trick:* Three strikeouts in same game. *Golden Sombrero:* Four strikeouts in same game. *Slump:* Lack of hits. *Drought:* Lack of runs. *Going to the Well:* Desperately needing a hit. *5 O'Clock Hitter:* Only performs in BP.

Pitching—Pulling Down the Shade: Throwing motion. *High T:* Formation after breaking ball from glove. *L:* Arm formation with ball above shoulder. *Arm Angle:* Either over-the-top, three-quarters, or sidearm. *Hurler, Chucker, Slinger:* Pitcher. *Wing:* Arm. *Ace, Stud, Number 1:* Top pitcher. *Southpaw:* Left-hander. *Power Pitcher:* Hard thrower. *Finesse Pitcher, Crafty:* Smart pitcher. *Stuff, Arsenal:* Repertoire. *Cheddar, Heat, Gas, Smoke, Velo:* Fast pitch. *Chin Music, Duster, Bean Ball:* Pitch high and inside. *Climb Ladder:* Pitch up in zone. *In the Kitchen, Jam, On Hands:* Pitching inside. *Comebacker:* Ground ball to mound. *K, Punch-Out, Throw Him a Chair, Whiff:* Strikeout. *Junk, Funny Stuff, Change-of-Pace:* Off-speed pitch. *Deuce, Bender, Hook, Hammer, Off the Table, Uncle Charlie, Yakker:* Breaking curveball. *Heavy Ball:* Sinking pitch. *Eephus:* Lob pitch. *Juiced:* Lively ball. *Doctored, Spit Ball:* Illegal pitches. *Dead, Scuffed:* Worn ball. *Paint the Black:* Work the corners.

On a Dime, In the Keyhole: Precise location. *Movement, Dancing, Tail:* Rotation of ball according to grip, release angle, or velocity. *Pitcher's Pitch:* Favorite pitch. *Out Pitch:* Two-strike pitch. *Waste, Pitch Around:* Predetermined non-strike. *Challenge, Payoff:* 3-and-2 pitch. *Pitchout:* Deliberate non-strike to catch base stealer. *Pickoff:* Throw from pitcher to an infielder. *Slide Step:* Quick stride to plate. *Spin Move, Step Off:* Defensive plays. *Quick Pitch:* Toss when batter is not ready. *In a Groove, Untouchable, Filthy:* Rate of success. *Gem:* Great performance. *No-No:* No-hitter. *Put Out Fire:* Stop rally. *Goose Egg:* No runs allowed. *Bullpen:* Warm-up area. *Closer, Fireman:* Reliever who closes out game. *Set-Up Man:* Person before closer. *Long Man:* Pitcher in blowout. *Submariner:* Throws underhand. *Rubber Arm:* Can pitch often. *Cy Young Award:* Top pitcher in each league. *Rolaids Award:* Top reliever. *Save:* Statistic awarded to reliever in close win. *Balk:* Illegal movement while on rubber. *ERA:* Total earned runs divided by innings then multiplying by nine. *Mistake, Hanger, Floater, Grooved:* Pitch left in hitting zone. *Meat, Flat, Rag Arm:* Ineffective. *Give 'Em a Compass, Wild Thing, Betty Itcher:* Erratic. *Running on Fumes* or *Empty, Put a Fork in Him, On the Ropes:* Need new pitcher. *Dead* or *Bum Arm:* Fatigue. *Hit the Showers, Hooked:* Knocked out of game. *Pitcher's Poison:* Get ball to the pitcher for a force out.

Fielding—Pickle: Rundown. *Around the Horn:* Throwing base to base. *Hot Corner:* Third baseman. *Backstop, General:* Catcher. *Stretch:* Lunge to reach throw. *Soft Hands, Flash Leather:* Good fielding technique. *Nose for Ball:* Good instincts. *Ball Hawk:* Great range. *Vacuum:* Flawless fielder. *Cat:* Quick fielder. *Tight D:* Good defense. *Gun, Hose:* Strong arm. *Dart:* Strong throw. *Lollipop, Dying Quail:* Weak throw. *Mustard, Zip, Fire, Air It Out, Uncork It:* Effort on throw. *Cutoff:* Relay throw. *Piggyback:* Double cutoff. *Crow-Hop:* Skip and throw. *Flip:* Bare hand toss. *Shoestring, Snow Cone, Basket, Snap, Circus, Routine:* Types of catches. *Charity Hop:* Easy bounce. *Can of Corn, In Back Pocket:* Routine catch. *Frame:* Good glove work by catcher. *Daylight:* Space between fielder and runner. *On the Grass:* Infielders playing in. *Double Play, Spin a Pair, Inning-Killer, One Plus One:* Two successive outs. *Phantom:* Missed tag. *Deek:* Defensive fake. *Backdoor:* Infielder slipping behind runner. *Trail:* Infielder following behind runner. *Cat and*

Mouse: Playing just behind runner. *Shift, Cheat:* Defensive movement according to the hitter. *Umbrella:* Corner infielders playing off the line. *Flash, Timing Play:* Pickoff plays. *Hidden Ball:* Trick play. *Wheel:* Infielder rotation in bunt situation. *E, Boot, Muff:* Error. *5-Hole, Through the Wickets:* Ball going between legs. *Infield Fly Rule:* Automatic out during force out situation with less than two outs.

Running—Jets, Wheels, Blur, Fleet Of Foot, Runs Like a Deer: Speed. *Slug, Molasses, Treading Water, Running with a Piano:* Slow. *Get Dirty:* Slide. *Hook, Headfirst, Pop-Up:* Types of slides. *Belly Up, Leave Your Feet:* Dive. *Raspberry:* Sliding burn. *Delay, Early:* Steal plays. *Station-to-Station:* Operating base to base. *Contact Play:* Running on contact at third base. *Freeze:* React to play. *Duck On Pond:* Runner on base. *Chicken:* Illegal play when leading is not allowed. *Hop:* Hustle. *Ghost Runner:* Invisible base runner. *Speed-Up Rule:* Running for catcher. *Blow:* Break from running.

Equipment—Pearl, Pill, Nugget, Rock, Nut, Egg: Ball. *Lumber, Club, Stick, Weapon, Wand:* Bat. *Gamer:* Favorite bat. *Lid, Cap:* Hat. *Spikes:* Cleats. *Stirrups:* Colored socks. *Breadbasket:* Large mitt. *Armor:* Catching gear. *L-Screen:* Protective pitching net. *Turtle:* Portable backstop. *Stretch Cord:* Rubber tubing. *Hollywoods:* Stationary bases. *Tee:* Stationary batting tool. *Donut, Bratt's Bat:* Weighted hitting devices. *Thunderstick:* Thin practice bat. *Fungo:* Bat used to hit grounders and fly balls. *Jugs:* Pitching machine or ball. *RIF:* Reduced Injury Factor ball. *Safe-T-Ball, Incrediball, Mush Ball, Rag Ball, Radar Ball:* Practice/indoor balls. *Boned:* Hardened wooden bat. *Corked:* Illegal bat. *War Paint:* Eye black. *Shades, Flip-Downs:* Sunglasses. *Rosin:* Drying powder. *Pine Tar:*

Sticky substance used for batting grip. *Radar Gun:* Device to read pitching velocity. *Laundry List:* Lineup card.

Other Sayings—Regular: Non-pitcher. *2-Way Player:* Hits and pitches. *Battery:* Pitcher and catcher. *5-Tool Player:* Hits for average and power, can run, throw and field. *Natural:* Seemingly effortless skills. *Spark Plug, Stirrin' in the Henhouse, Open Flood Gates, Leaky Dam:* Rally. *Smokin':* Very successful. *Money:* Clutch. *Curtain Call:* Acknowledge cheers from dugout. *Tip of Cap:* Give credit to opposition. *DL:* Disabled list. *Riding Pine, Splinters:* Sitting on bench. *Pink Slip, Waived, Released, Designated for Assignment:* Cut. *Dead Time:* In between the action. *In Between the Lines:* Actual game playing. *Follow Through:* Final stage of a swing or pitch. *Adjustment:* Adapting to competition. *Like-, Opposite-Handed:* Arm-batter scenario. *Tunnel Vision, Zone In, Bear Down:* Focus. *Double Switch:* Substituting two players for pitcher's spot. *Re-Entry:* Substitution without leaving game. *Little Things:* Not relating to fundamentals. *Little Ball:* Getting on base and making every hit count. *Ring Up, Bang Out:* Out. *Guns, Pipes:* Muscles. *Scrapper:* Aggressive. *Nails, Bulldog:* Tough. *Loose Cannon, Tapped, Screw Loose:* Crazy. *Empty the Tank:* Effort. *Gut It Out, Walking Wounded, Dinged:* Play hurt. *Hot Dog, Showboat:* Cocky. *The Show, Bigs:* Major Leagues. *The Farm, Bushes:* Minors. *Rookie, A, AA, AAA:* Levels of minor leagues. *Independent League:* Professional baseball unaffiliated with the majors. *Grapefruit League:* Spring training. *Winter League:* Baseball played outside U.S. during winter months. *Opening Day:* First game. *Twin Bill, Double Dip:* Doubleheader. *Rubber Game:* Deciding game of split series. *Sweep:* Consecutive wins in series. *Under the Candles:* Night game. *Take Me Out to the Ball Game:* Official baseball anthem. *7th Inning Stretch:* Time to get up and move around. *Midsummer Classic:* All-Star Game. *Dog Days of Summer:* Games in late August. *Barn Burner, Donnybrook:* Close game. *Pennant Race:* Close competition at end of season. *Magic Number:* Wins needed for postseason. *The Dance:* Play-offs. *Fall Classic:* World Series. *Cellar, Second Division:* Bottom of league. *Barnstorm:* Play all day. *Hot Stove:* Winter meetings. *Dugout:* Bench area. *Clubhouse:* Locker room. *Bunting:* Decorative flags hung on Opening Day or in play-offs. *Hardware:* Trophies. *Blue:* Umpire. *Skipper:* Manager. *Brain Trust:* Coaching staff. *Indicator:* Tip-off for signal. *Wipe:* Play is off. *Letters:* Upper chest area on uniform. *Strike Zone:* Letters to knees. *Tight* or *Wide Zone:* Umpire's strike zone. *Line Score:* Runs, hits and errors. *Pitching* or *Spray Chart:* Noting player results. *Indian Rubber:* Runner is out when hit by thrown ball. *Bleacher Bum:* Fan in outfield stands. *Bronx Cheer:* Booing from fans. *Rubber Necks:* press. *Red Hot:* Hot dog. *Rinse Out:* Water break.

I leave you with three questions to ponder:
1. What is the origin behind the name of the game "Pepper"?
2. Why is the foul pole *not* called the fair pole?
3. Why haven't the Cubs been able to win a World Series since 1908?

Index of Games
and Activities

Action Ball 95–96
Air Raid 82
All World Hitting 100
Anything Goes 73–74
Around the Horn 69
Axe Bat 90–91

Back-Up 66–67
Backwards Baseball 123
Balancing Act 31
Ball Tag 167
Baseball Gags 170–171
Baseball Played With
  Re-Entry Rule 128
Baseball Quizzes
  171–172
Baseball/Softball Golf
  136
Basics of Baserunning
  24–25
Basics of Bunting
  42–43
Basics of Catching
  50–51
Basics of Fielding
  56–57
Basics of Hitting 88–89
Basics of Throwing and
  Pitching 142–143

Bat Flip 78
Batting Practice
  108–109
Beat Ball 157
Besuboru 92
Biathlon 124–125
Big Bertha 91–92
Big Mac 92–93
Billy Ball 111–112
La Boca 81
Body Double 135
Bone Rack 72–73
Box 154
Box Drill 70–71
Break the Tape 28
Bucket 29
Bull's-Eye 148

Charlie Hustle 37
Color Coded Hitting
  94–95
Colorful 153–154
Combat 112–113
Copy Cat 81
Court Ball 159–160
Crab Ball 120
Crash Dummy 85
Crazed 35–36
Cutoff 60–61

Dart Baseball 170
Dash for Cash 29–30
Dean the Dummy 150–
  151
Department Store 33–
  34
Dinger Ball 98–99
Dizzy Bat Race 30
Dome Ball 101
Don't Miss 96–97
Donut 95
D.R. 124
Dump 75–76

Elimination 147–148
Elway Drill 62
Every Which Way 110–
  111

Fielding Relays 64
Flip 77–78
Four-Way Bunting 47
Four-Way Grounders
  59–60
Fox Trot 38

Game Attractions 172–
  173
Gas Master 134–135

German Baseball 158–159
Goalie 65–66
Golden Chuck Bat 126–127
Good Olde Days 124–125
Green Monster 62–63
Grip It 146
Gun It 152

Have a Ball 72
Heave-Ho 155–156
Hey Batter, Batter 121
Hit the Bat 168
Hit the Fielder 100–101
Hitters Challenge 99–100
Hole in One 43–44
Home Run Derby 97–98
Horn 32
Hose Master 167–168
Hot Potato 161
Hurry Up 117–118

I Got It 68–69
In Your Ear 102
Infield-Outfield 58–59
Intrasquad 127

Juggling 77
Junk Ball 114–116

Kick Softball 86
King Cone 69–70
Knockout 80

Last Man 65
Liberty Bell 34–35
Liner 103

Mafisto 82–83
Magician 89–90
Mano y Mano 104
Mini Di 63–64
Missile 167
Mission Impossible 64–65
Mosquito 85

Move It 44–45
Movement 146–147

Name That Play 108

Olympiad 137–138
One Toss 79–80
Opposite 122–123
Orbit 71

Peas 46
Pepper 104–105
P.F.P. 67–68
Pickups 31–32
Pinball 46
Pitcher's Practice 149–150
Pointer 61–62
Punch Ball 156–157
Pyramid 169

Que Pasa? 63

Radar 162
Rain 52
Rain Delay 169–170
Rebound 155
Relay 61
Relay Races 30–31
Right Field 119
Rip 101–102
Road Block 52
Rock Ball 105–106
Run Home 119–120

Sandlot 111
Scamper 27
See, Read & Explode 93
Seven Hundred Club 73
Shadow Ball 76
Shaggy 110
Shin Guard Shuffle 53
Showcase 130–133
Slow-Pitch Softball 166–167
Smelly Sock 103–104
Soft Toss 94
Speed Trap 32–33

Splinter 106–107
Stadium Shot 98
Staff Day 150
Stand-Up 120–121
Starter 28–29
Steak Dinner 114
Stickball 114
Stoopball 80–81
Strike Zone 148
Super Catch 69
Superman 83–84
Survivor 138–139

T-Ball 125
T-Drill 151
Target Practice 107–108
Team Baserunning Drills 25–26
Team Bunting Drills 43
Team Catching Drills 51
Team Hitting Drills 89
Team Infield Drills 57–58
Team Outfield Drills 58
Team Pitching Drills 144–146
Team Throwing Drills 144
Tee Ball 111
Tennis Baseball 136–137
Three-Two-One 166
Throw Ball 156
Tic-Tac-Toe 37
Tools of the Trade 38–39
Touch Base Relay 27
Touch 'Em All 26–27
Tournament 128–130
Town Ball 123–124
Train 60
Treasure Hunt 86
Twelfth Man 133–134
Twenty-One 161
Two Ball 79

Ultimate Pickle 84–85
Ultimate Throw & Catch 162–163
Umpire 153

Vamos! 36

Wall Ball 158
W.A.N.D.Y. 135–136
Whack 126
Wiffle ball 116–117

W.I.G. 121–122
Wig the Bat 163–164
Wig the Coach 164–165
Wig the Cone 165
Win It 113
Windex 118–119

Wisk 34
Wrist Hitting 91

You Field It 74–75
You-Me 66